KINVER & ENVILLE

THE PHOTOGRAPHIC COLLECTION

BOB CLARKE, TONY FREER & MICHAEL REUTER

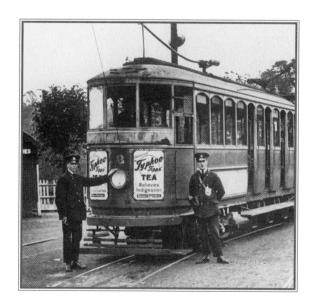

SUTTON PUBLISHING LIMITED

This edition first published in 2003 by
Sutton Publishing Limited • Phoenix Mill
Thrupp • Stroud • Gloucestershire • GL5 2BU

Kinver & Enville in Old Photographs was first published in 1996 by Sutton Publishing Limited
Kinver & Enville in Old Photographs: A Second Selection was first published in 1998 by Sutton
Publishing Limited

British Library Cataloguing in Publication Data
A catalogue record for this book is available from the British Library.

ISBN 0 7509 3357 7

Typeset in 10.5/13.5 Photina.
Typesetting and origination by
Sutton Publishing Limited.
Printed and bound in England by
J.H. Haynes & Co. Ltd, Sparkford.

KINVER & ENVILLE

The Photographic Collection

CONTENTS

Part One – Kinver & Enville

Part Two – Kinver & Enville: A Second Selection

THE BLACK COUNTRY SOCIETY

The Black Country Society is proud to be associated with **Sutton Publishing** of Stroud. In 1994 the society was invited by Sutton Publishing to collaborate in what has proved to be a highly successful publishing partnership, namely the extension of the *Britain in Old Photographs* series into the Black Country. In this joint venture the Black Country Society has played an important role in establishing and developing a major contribution to the region's photographic archives by encouraging society members to compile books of photographs of the area or town in which they live.

The first book in the Black Country series was *Wednesbury in Old Photographs* by Ian Bott, launched by Lord Archer of Sandwell in November 1994. Since then 55 Black Country titles have been published. The total number of photographs contained in these books is in excess of 11,000, suggesting that the whole collection is probably the largest regional photographic survey of its type in any part of the country to date.

This voluntary society, affiliated to the Civic Trust, was founded in 1967 as a reaction to the trends of the late 1950s and early '60s. This was a time when the reorganisation of local government was seen as a threat to the identity of individual communities and when, in the name of progress and modernisation, the industrial heritage of the Black Country was in danger of being swept away.

The general aims of the society are to stimulate interest in the past, present and future of the Black Country, and to secure at regional and national levels an accurate understanding and portrayal of what constitutes the Black Country and, wherever possible, to encourage and facilitate the preservation of the Black Country's heritage.

The society, which now has over 2,500 members worldwide, organises a yearly programme of activities. There are six venues in the Black Country where evening meetings are held on a monthly basis from September to April. In the summer months, there are fortnightly guided evening walks in the Black Country and its green borderland, and there is also a full programme of excursions further afield by car. Details of all these activities are to be found on the society's website, **www.blackcountrysociety.co.uk**, and in *The Blackcountryman*, the quarterly magazine that is distributed to all members.

PO Box 71 · Kingswinford · West Midlands DY6 9YN

PART ONE

KINVER & ENVILLE
IN OLD PHOTOGRAPHS

If you are **FED** with everything **UP** come to **KINVER.**

"THEO"

INTRODUCTION

Today's village of Kinver, in modern parlance a 'large' village of some 8,000 people, first made an appearance in 736 AD as 'Cynibre', the name relating to a woodland. In 964 the area was known as 'Cynfare' (a Royal road) and in the Domesday Book of 1086 as 'Chenevare' (a great ridge or edge), King's land and in which there were two mills and a manor.

Despite being close to what was to become the Black Country and, from the 17th century to the mid-19th century with a flourishing iron working industry powered by the River Stour, it still managed to avoid the spread of industry and housing. Instead it developed into a self-contained community which today maintains its individuality having successfully resisted the continuing expansion of the West Midland conurbation.

There is no doubt that in remaining an individual, if not a unique community, Kinver has been helped by its geographic location set amidst hilly countryside, separated from the encroaching suburbs by an arterial road, a river, a canal and, most importantly, surrounded by green belt land with much of the village being a designated conservation area.

From its origins as a Royal Hunting forest and being within one of the most scenically attractive areas in the Midlands, Kinver attracted many wealthy and influential landowners, several of whom were associated with the wool and, later, iron industries.

However, with the decline of the iron working industry in the 19th century, the village population fell as many families moved out to work in the flourishing industries of the Black Country or emigrated overseas.

Kinver as we know it today began to develop at the turn of the 20th century with the arrival of the Kinver Light Railway, offering a cheap and reliable transport system. Thus the first steps in the commuter age began and, at the same time, Kinver's unique rural attraction came within economic reach of tens of thousands of people who eagerly took the opportunity 'for a day out in the country'.

Although Kinver in some respects came to be regarded (and still is) as a dormitory area for Black Country industry and commerce, the village managed to retain its own identity and develop a thriving tourist industry. By the time the railway closed, Kinver had a regular bus service to Stourbridge and many coach operators were quick to capitalize on Kinver's attraction as a day and half-day excursion venue. With the arrival of the motor car, especially since 1950, Kinver has maintained its popularity. The great escarpment of Kinver Edge, the remains of its Iron Age fort earthworks and its National Trust heathland, the woods and rock houses all tower above the village to give it a special appeal to visitors and inhabitants alike.

In the following pages a century of the development of an unpretentious country village into a lively and diverse community, which still retains the essentials of English village life, is traced in words and photographs.

CHAPTER ONE

THE KINVER LIGHT RAILWAY

Opened in 1901, the Kinver Light Railway ran from the Fish Inn, Amblecote (Stourbridge) to Kinver, until 1930 when it fell victim to competition from road transport and closed.

More popularly known as 'the Kinver Trams', these vehicles carried thousands of day-trippers from the Black Country and Birmingham during their comparatively short life. By the time buses, cars and coaches made their appearance, Kinver had become a major venue for people escaping from the grime and smoke of the Black Country for a day out 'in the country'. Leaving Amblecote, the line travelled through Wollaston and along the Bridgnorth Road to the Stewponey and Foley Arms Hotel, Stourton. From there it crossed the Staffordshire and Worcestershire Canal and the River Stour to begin its journey through meadows and woodland to Kinver village.

A scene at the Stewponey & Foley Arms Hotel shortly after the tramway opened in 1901, where pedestrians, ponies and traps await the arrival (far left) of the tram from Amblecote to Kinver. The reference to 'Foley Arms' relates to the Foley family who, having made a vast fortune from the iron working industry in the Stour Valley and Black Country, became generous benefactors to many worthy causes in the area.

Changing times, *c.* 1920. The age of the motor car had arrived, a new licensee, Mr Berry, was mine host at the Stewponey, trees had begun to grow on the forecourt, the flagpole had disappeared and, although still operating, the line was carrying fewer passengers.

When the line closed in 1930, its bridge over the canal was demolished and a new road bridge carrying the A458 Bridgnorth Road was built on roughly the same site.

Next stop, Kinver . . . Hyde Meadows Halt, *c.* 1909, was the last stop before the Kinver terminus. Note the old tramcar body converted into a waiting room. Hyde Meadows is still a pleasant country walk from the village.

Three modes of transport, *c.* 1926. While a lone walker uses the towing path, an Amblecote-bound tram emerges from woodland at The Hyde and a horse-drawn narrowboat, loaded with Black Country coal, heads towards Kidderminster and Stourport.

A variety of tramcars were used on the line. In the summer months, the quaintly named 'toast racks' – on account of their open sides – allowed passengers to breathe in the fresh air after leaving the Black Country.

When the line opened in 1901, the site of the former Hyde Iron Works was used as the railway's winter storage depot. A car is pictured about to leave The Hyde depot on a service run.

The Light Railway carried more than just passengers. This picture of the Kinver Terminus, c. 1908, shows milk churns about to be loaded into the car. To the left is the parcels and ticket office; by all accounts, an invaluable service for the quick and relatively cheap carriage of parcels and other small items was offered.

Tram Terminus, Kinver

Immediately the line opened, the village's fortunes changed for the better. With the collapse of the local iron industry, many families emigrated to the booming industry of the Black Country; some went even further – to the 'new worlds' of America, Canada, South Africa and Australia. For those remaining in Kinver, to work in Stourbridge or Amblecote meant walking or cycling at least 4 miles each way, there being no public transport. The line was an immediate success. Not only did it stem the tide of the population drifting away from the village but it brought many day trippers into Kinver – which the company's publicity literature described as 'the Switzerland of the Midlands'.

This picture was taken in about 1905, at the peak of the line's success in passenger numbers. On Whitsuntide Monday and Tuesday 1905, the line brought over 31,000 people into the village in a thirty-hour period. Contemporary reports tell of queues of homeward-bound day trippers stretching back into the High Street with trams travelling at seven-minute intervals. So popular had Kinver and 'The Edge' become that through services began running from places further afield such as Dudley and West Bromwich.

Thus Kinver took the first steps to becoming something of a 'dormitory' area for Black Country industry and commerce and a weekend-away-from-it-all resort. Indeed many industrialists built weekend cottages on the fringe of the village or bought existing houses there.

CHAPTER TWO

STAFFORDSHIRE & WORCESTERSHIRE CANAL

The Staffordshire & Worcestershire Canal was part of James Brindley's 'Grand Cross' of canals linking the Severn, Trent, Mersey and Thames rivers together. It leaves the Trent & Mersey Canal at Great Haywood, near Stafford, and joins the River Severn at Stourport. Its opening in 1772 brought immediate economic benefits to Kinver in the form of cheaper bulk transport of raw materials such as coal, timber and other commodities.

With the opening of the Stourbridge Canal a few years later to Stourton Junction which, in turn, was connected to the Dudley Canal, the Staffordshire and Worcestershire Canal became one of the busiest and most prosperous waterways in the country as Black Country industry sent its goods to the Severn and on to Gloucester and Avonmouth Docks for export. Commercial carrying had all but ceased in 1950, but by 1960 privately owned and holiday hire-boats were making their appearance. By the 1990s the canal was once again one of the busiest on the waterway network and was carrying more pleasure craft than it did cargo boats 200 years before.

Hyde Lock and Cottage has always been one of the most popular subjects for artists and photographers and, apart from surrounding tree growth, has changed little over the last century. The house in the distance was once part of The Hyde Iron Works complex.

Equally timeless is Dunsley Dell, *c.* 1906, the bridle path from Dunsley to The Hyde, possibly an ancient pack-horse trail.

Kinver Lock, *c.* 1906. In front of the building on the right was a weighbridge whilst beyond that was the Lock Inn, believed to have been built shortly after the canal was opened in 1772, primarily as a boatman's pub. At the side of the later Vine Inn was an access road to a wharf operated by William Walker & Sons, which now forms part of the Vine Inn's beer garden. At a point behind the camera was a crane and wharf, while on the Dunsley side of the canal below the lock were another two wharves, reflecting the amount of waterborne trade from Kinver and district until around 1920 by which time road transport was becoming well established.

Shropshire Union Railway Boat *Wilden* pictured in about 1910 after having worked through Kinver Lock. The railway company concerned was the LNWR (later the LMS), which had taken control of the Shropshire Union Canal from Wolverhampton to Chester to give it a transport route through GWR territory.

A sign of the times, *c.* 1960. An unkempt Kinver Lock reflected the likelihood of the eventual closure of the canal by the British Transport Commission – a proposal which was rapidly withdrawn after a public outcry. Ironically, the boat pictured here was one of British Transport (Waterways) own holiday hire fleet.

RALTAR, KINVER

This postcard view, *c.* 1930, of the canal from Kinver bridge shows in the foreground a 'day boat' owned by the Staffordshire, Worcestershire and Shropshire Electric Power Company (popularly known as the SWS), laden with coal and bound for the new power station at Stourport, opened in 1928. Because of their destination, all boats in this trade were known by boatmen as 'light boats' and were usually crewed by Black Countrymen who tied up at night either at Stourton or Kinver, went home by tram (and later, bus) returning early next morning to continue the journey, their horses usually being stabled locally. The coal came mainly from Ashwood Basin (now a boating marina) where the Earl of Dudley's private railway brought coal from his collieries to the canalside wharves. This traffic ceased almost overnight when, in 1948, following the nationalization of the railways and canals, all the coal traffic was switched to rail when British Railways opened a branch into the power station from the main line at Stourport.

How the area known as Gibraltar got its name is debatable. Possibly the outcrop of sandstone which became a cliff-face when the canal was cut had something to do with it, as the name was in existence in 1780. This scene of 1908 shows a number of houses perched on the hillside. According to a history of the local Methodist Church, the Wesleyans held services in a 'rock house' at Gibraltar in 1846, prior to which they had been holding meetings in the Lock Inn. By 1830 there were twelve rock houses, with seventeen being recorded in 1851. Many inhabitants were employed on the local canal wharves. Although the houses were deemed unhealthy in 1880, many continued to be used for a number of years by boatmen.

CHAPTER THREE

THE RIVER STOUR

Looking at the River Stour today, it is difficult, if not impossible, to imagine it as a navigable waterway. Yet in 1667 it was passable from Stourbridge to Kidderminster thanks to the efforts of Andrew Yarranton, and coal was carried from Stourbridge and Amblecote to Kidderminster.

Yarranton's plan was to make the river navigable to Lower Mitton in Stourport and he received Parliamentary approval for such a scheme in 1662. Finances ran out by the time he had reached Kidderminster and when, around 1670, a freak storm wrecked the navigation works, repairs were not undertaken and the navigation was abandoned.

For centuries the Stour's banks were home to many mills of various types and there were five in Kinver alone. Where weirs had been built to impound the water, the river was also used for pleasure boating. Eventually the weirs either collapsed or were removed and the river reverted to its natural state; years later extensive dredging saw spoil being piled against the banks making the river much narrower. At the same time industrial pollution from Black Country industries killed off all water life and the Stour had the dubious distinction of being one of the most polluted rivers in the country.

Today, however, thanks to anti-pollution measures, the river is slowly cleansing itself and several varieties of coarse fish have returned to its waters.

At the turn of the last century Mr John Timmings operated a 'boating station' from the Mill Pool, Mill Lane. Unfortunately all boating activity ended when the mill weir deteriorated and the river level dropped. The site is now occupied by the Mill House sheltered accommodation for the elderly. The identities of the three men pictured are not known.

Mr Timmings's steam launch with passengers negotiating one of the many sharp bends in the river. Whilst a canopy can be seen protecting the helmsman and 'engineer' from the elements, the passengers did not seem to have such a luxury! Mr Timmings also ran a larger launch (below), which was capable of carrying up to twenty-five passengers.

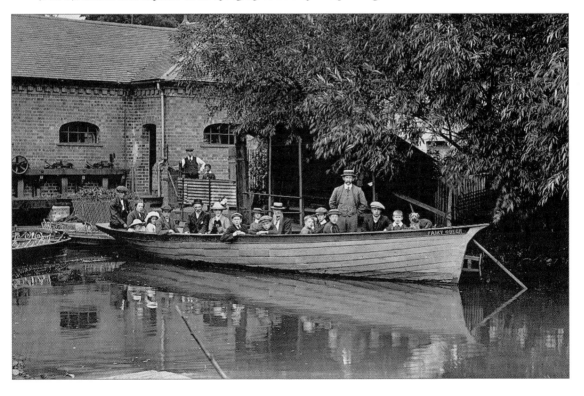

A pleasant summer afternoon's boating and fishing on the Stour adjoining the village. A far cry from today's narrow river channel and high banks.

Boating and Fishing.
River Stour, Kinver.

The river level at Kinver can rise rapidly at times of heavy rainfall in the Stour Valley and, as this photograph taken from near the Lock Inn around 1920 shows, flood water closed Mill Lane to all except horsedrawn traffic.

The old river bridge with the Stag Inn in the background, *c.* 1910.

With the increasing number and size of vehicles travelling in and out of Kinver, it became evident that a wider and stronger bridge was needed. This work was carried out in 1921.

The new bridge ready for the onslaught of the motor car. . . .

CHAPTER FOUR

HIGH STREET

Kinver village was described by Stebbing Shaw in 'History and Antiquities of Staffordshire', in 1798 as 'one long spacious street well paved with pebbles'. Over 500 years earlier Kinver had been given a formal Borough Charter, and as there are no records of that title ever having been removed, Kinver could still feasibly refer to itself as a Borough.

That 'one long spacious street' also encompassed the Borough and eventually became known as High Street; today its architecture spans some 500 years and not even the continual presence of road traffic can completely overcome that sense of history.

As will be revealed in the following pages, many of the properties have their own stories to tell. Collectively these stories are the history of a village.

By the time this postcard appeared in 1923, Kinver was a well-established tourist venue. This view of High Street, taken from the junction of Church Hill and Mill Lane, shows 'E. Guttery' offering teas and 'apartments' – obviously in competition with the Temperance Hotel next door. These two properties were demolished around 1946.

Further evidence of enterprising Kinver residents cashing in on the early 20th-century tourist boom. On the right is Kemp's Refreshment and Tea Rooms, roughly on the site of today's Spar Supermarket. On the left, three of the four villas (which still exist) were offering tourist facilities including accommodation.

The name 'Burgesses', by which this house was known, dates back several hundred years to the time when the Lord of the Manor issued a 'Charter of Liberties for his Burgesses', and at the same time created the Borough of Kinver. The Borough was an area of land encompassing what is now both sides of the High Street. The house was demolished in the early 1960s but its name was retained for the area now occupied by sheltered accommodation for the elderly.

Apart from the disappearance of the Temperance Hotel on the right and the cottages on the left, the remainder of the High Street has changed little since this photograph from the mid-1930s.

High Street viewed from outside the Constitutional Club, *c.* 1960. The Co-operative Society moved out of the village for a number of years but reappeared in time for the twenty-first century.

High Street in 1909, and the only vehicles in sight are a horsedrawn cart and, on the right-hand pavement a pedal cycle. The building in the centre background was built in 1851 as a National School for Boys and Girls. A separate school for girls was built in 1873; the building is now the library. A boys' school was built in Castle Street and the older building then used as an infants' school.

One of the most distinctive façades of any property in High Street is The Pharmacy. For 140 years it has been the village's pharmacy, while for over fifty years the other section of the building (right) was the village post office – as seen in this picture, *c.* 1910. Previously the post office had been at 33 High Street, moving to the Pharmacy building in around 1908.

A photograph (above) taken some fifty years later shows little change apart from a weighing machine outside Mr Bills's Pharmacy and a post office sign. With the growth in demand for telephones in Kinver in the 1950s, the telephone exchange became overloaded and a new fully automatic exchange was built at Dunsley. A mobile crane was then used to remove the old exchange equipment (below) via a first floor window.

Possibly a Saturday afternoon in 1911, with people enjoying a stroll down an almost traffic-free High Street. Many would have been day-trippers who had come to Kinver on the Light Railway from the Black Country. This postcard could have been a publicity photograph for the newsagent, Mr Jennings, whose name on the shop blind seems to have been enhanced for the benefit of clarity. Although this card was published in about 1920, it is a reprint of a 1911 postcard when the newsagent's shop blind carried the name 'Morgan'. To the right of centre foreground can be seen a uniformed man, possibly the village police constable. The very wide road and pavements at this point, the junction of High Street and Vicarage Drive, mark the area in which the village Bull Ring was situated and also the site of the 17th-century Market House, which, by all accounts, was short-lived.

An almost deserted High Street in 1906 gives a clear view of the ancient frontage of the White Harte Hotel which, as licensed premises, has existed since 1605. High Street once carried the main Bristol–Chester road and the White Harte was a well-patronized hostelry. Evidence of Civil War activity around Kinver is well documented and, during restoration work at the hotel, a Cromwellian helmet was discovered. In the early 19th century the hotel was the venue for the 'Borough Meeting' and in 1830 there are records of a 'White Harte Club', which may have been an early version of a Friendly Society.

Despite substantial local opposition, the Alms Houses in High Street were demolished in the 1960s and replaced with a modern shop development. Ten years later such demolition would have been unlikely as the centre of the village had been designated a conservation area.

The date of this picture is unknown but it could be of a parade marking the end of the Second World War. To the right, the group of marching men may have been either Auxiliary Police ('Specials'), Auxiliary Fire Service or Air Raid Wardens. Behind them are drummers wearing what appears to have been army uniforms – could they be the Home Guard? Kinver Historical Society would be grateful if anyone could identify the occasion.

For years Mr Archie Taylor was the village's hairdresser; he was also the founder of the Village Band. Stories are told of customers being attended to while band practice proceeded in a back room and then having to wait while Mr Taylor rushed into the practice room to berate some hapless bandsman for blowing a wrong note!

Kinver Tea Stores receiving a delivery of provisions, *c.* 1905. The wagon was owned by a Joseph Norton of Wolverhampton. (Facing page, top) The Tea Stores had been taken over by Mr Sid Phillips, pictured here in 1958 demonstrating the ultimate in customer service by giving Pauline Beebee a 'piggy-back' across the flooded High Street. Mrs Phillips is seen in the side entry door. (Below) An internal view of the shop, with Mrs Dorothy Day serving Mrs I. Williams, *c.* 1960.

A view of High Street looking towards Church Hill, *c.* 1910.

The first of many newsagents (Morgan, Jennings and now Stars News Shops) was Miss Dorothy Ellen Lizzie Taylor. This photograph of about 1914 shows the newspaper billboard announcing the size of the German army and the declaration of war.

High Street, 1964 (above). The building on the extreme right was formerly the Red Lion pub, later changing to an English and now a Chinese restaurant.

The cottages and shops on the left were demolished and the land used for a car-park. In 1992 and in the teeth of some local opposition, the Normid Housing Association built a block of apartments here, which won an architecture and design award as well as an award from the Kinver Civic Society.

Although not in the High Street, Harris's Garage of Stone Lane was strategically placed on the main route used by motorists and cyclists heading towards Kinver Edge from High Street. Mr Harris lost no time in offering parking for cars and motorcycle combinations for 6*d*, motor cycles 4*d* and cycles 2*d*. He also served refreshments. His petrol was delivered by hand operated pumps. Note the sign 'battery charging station' – the days when, before everyone had electricity, people with wireless sets powered them by accumulators which were charged from the mains supply.

CHAPTER FIVE

LICENSED PREMISES

Although being classed as a large village with a population of around 8,000, the original village's central area has retained much of its character by reason of the river and a backdrop of hills.

As a result – and because of the influx of visitors which is now experienced throughout the year rather than in just the summer months – comparatively few pubs have closed down.

In recent years Kinver gained national fame when it was listed by CAMRA Real Ale Guide as well worth a visit for good quality and value. Most of the pubs now provide meals and, as the village's tourist trade has increased, a number of licensed restaurants have become established, two of which began life as pubs.

Arguably the best-known hostelry from a historical point of view within Kinver parish is the Whittington Inn standing on the A449 Kidderminster–Wolverhampton road. But it was not until the 18th century that it became licensed property; before that it was the manor house of the De Whittingtons, having been built in about 1310. Richard, a grandson of the first owner, eventually became Lord Mayor of London on four occasions. His background of some aristocracy destroys the story of him arriving in London, poor and penniless, with his cat and then making his fortune.

The Inn has several links with royalty: Lady Jane Grey spent some of her childhood there; King Charles II is reputed to have stayed there during his flight from Worcester (Kinver is one place where he didn't climb a tree!); and in 1711 Queen Anne called and, as was her custom when staying overnight, left her iron seal (since stolen) on the door.

The interior of the Whittington Inn is what today's traveller would expect from a building of such antiquity. Above is the heavily timbered lounge hall whilst below is the bedroom used by Lady Jane Grey when she lived there as a child. Her ghost is said to still roam the corridors. . . .

The Stag Inn, Mill Lane when a Mr J. Blakeway, Home Brewer, was the licensee, *c.* 1904. It has long since been demolished. The inn was conveniently situated almost opposite the Kinver Light Railway terminus. Beyond the Stag is a row of cottages standing against the sandstone cliff adjoining The Holloway. The occupants carved caves out of the sandstone and used them as outhouses and storerooms. With the cottages long gone, the caves can now be seen in their entirety.

White Hill in 1917 was a scene of almost open countryside. The building to the right was formerly The Spring Gardens, rebuilt as pictured as The Spring. In about 1938 it was demolished and replaced by The New Rose & Crown to serve the growing residential development of Kinver. The land in the immediate foreground and almost up to the skyline was completely built over by the 1970s.

Formerly the Car & Horses, this building predated the arrival of the motor car by many years despite its name, the only explanation being that the word car was merely short for 'carriage'. It was completely refurbished as a house which became known as The Armoury, on the grounds that it had some connection with the Civil War – a claim that has never been substantiated either by artefacts or documentary evidence. This photograph is dated from around 1895.

The Green Dragon in High Street, seen above in about 1898, was first licensed in 1718. In about 1902 it was rebuilt as an upmarket hotel in anticipation of an influx of residential bookings which never materialized. In 1936 it became the Constitutional Club, its exterior virtually the same today – as depicted in the 1905 postcard below.

The Red Lion, today a Chinese restaurant, stood on the corner of what is now the access road to the public car-park known locally as The Acre. The photograph was taken pre-1900, for in 1896 Kelly's Directory named George Boswell as the licensee. With the Union Flag (Union Jack) flying, this photograph could have been taken at the time of Queen Victoria's Golden Jubilee of 1897. In 1900, Kelly's Directory named Giblum Grimshaw as licensee. At the rear of the Red Lion a Mr Underwood offered 'good stabling'. From the car-park a footpath leads up to the parish church.

High Street from near the Vine Café, *c.* 1895.

This 1912 postcard view of a near deserted High Street also heralded the arrival of road transport as a delivery van trundles past the Crown Inn on the left; this is now the Kinfayre Restaurant.

Known locally as 'The Steps' was the Mitchells & Butlers Pub, the Plough & Harrow, High Street as seen, *c*. 1950. It is now a Batham's House, well known for its real ale, Bathams being one of the few surviving true Black Country breweries. Next door (extreme right) can be seen the bricked-up window arch of the former Baptist chapel built in 1814. The chapel became an Anglican Sunday School in 1827, was returned to the Baptists in 1834 and was later let to the Primitive Methodists who remained there until 1839. Eventually it was converted into retail premises.

The Royal Exchange, Enville Road, *c.* 1912, was the setting for the group photograph above; whether it was a special event or merely a gathering of the 'regulars' is not recorded. The Royal Exchange was also known locally as 'The Cherry Tree' as can be seen from the photograph below, *c.* 1918, when Kinver was beginning to receive visits from motorists.

CHURCHES

From its hilltop position, the parish church dominates the village. It is possible that the area could have been a place of pagan worship before the arrival of Christianity. It is known that there was a priest in Kinver in 1086, although it was not until the 12th century that there was any record of a church building. Some of the present church's original Norman stonework still exists.

The hilltop position of the parish church can be seen perfectly in this 1930s postcard.

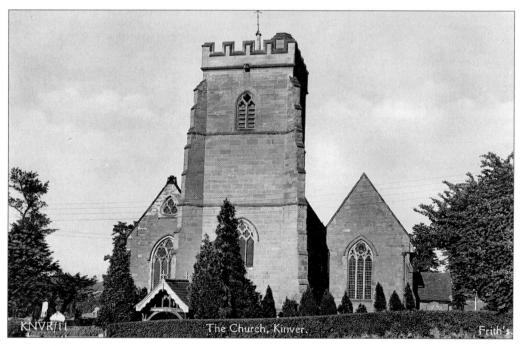

Kinver Church, seen here in about 1938, appears to have been rebuilt in the early 14th century and only fragments of stone survive from an earlier Norman construction. Over the past 600 years many alterations have been carried out on the building, a major external job being the demolition of the north aisle (left) in 1976, which had become structurally unsafe. It was replaced to a design by Mr J.G. Smith of Kinver.

In 1878 a restoration scheme was undertaken and spread over a number of years, the work finally being completed for Queen Victoria's Golden Jubilee celebrations in 1887. At the same time as the north aisle was being rebuilt in 1976, the wooden ceiling of the nave was removed to uncover the medieval roof.

Trinity Church (Wesleyan Methodist) was built in High Street in 1887 to a design by Isaac Meacham of Cradley Heath, who also designed the Sunday School Hall which was opened in 1889. The church closed in the early 1960s with the congregation joining the Methodists of Potter's Cross, Kinver. The buildings were then occupied for a time by youth organizations, but the cost of maintenance and the unwelcome attentions of local vandals led to demolition in 1995. The site was redeveloped as retirement homes.

At the turn of the last century, the Primitive Methodists obtained land at the junction of Meddins Lane and Enville Road, Potter's Cross, and built a chapel measuring 30 ft by 18 ft and made of corrugated metal sheeting. In this postcard view of Potter's Cross, *c.* 1920, the tiny chapel can be seen above the hedgerow. In 1924 the congregation built Christ Church on adjoining land in 1924, with the chapel then becoming a Sunday School.

The then modern style of church architecture can be seen in the Methodist Church, Potter's Cross, which was opened in 1961. With the closure of the Wesleyan Methodist Church, it became known as Kinver Methodist Church. Much of the cost of the new building came from a bequest made by Mr F. Payne of Norton, Stourbridge.

PRINCIPAL HOUSES

As becomes a long-established community set within particularly attractive rural surroundings, Kinver had several large and prestigious houses, many dating back several centuries and almost all of which remain in existence. Owners over the last 200 years reflect the popularity of Kinver amongst the successful industrialists, first those of the local ironworking industry and later, as transport links improved, of the Black Country. Several smaller houses were built by Black Country businessmen as weekend and holiday homes.

The origins of Prestwood House, situated off the A449 Wolverhampton–Kidderminster road, have been traced back to the reign of Richard III when it was occupied by John De Somery. It is said that even before this period the area was associated with members of a monastic order attached to the monastery at Wolverhampton. Over the centuries, many famous local families occupied and added to the house, among them being the Dudleys, Lytteltons, Sebrights, Hodgsons and Foleys. At the end of its life as a grand residence it became a sanatorium for victims of tuberculosis. It is now a private nursing home.

Prestwood House was, naturally, the venue for many social events such as the Hunt Meet (above) and a Rook Shoot (below), where a house party pose complete with their 'bag', *c.* 1907. The occupant of the house at that time was Mr George Salter, who can be seen at the centre of the front row.

Prestwood Estate covered a substantial area, and in this picture Miss Salter (left) is pictured with Miss Savery and a companion in a donkey cart before a morning ride, *c.* 1908.

The impressive Victorian and Edwardian furnishings of Mrs Salter's drawing room at Prestwood House, *c.* 1910.

In 1316, Dunsley Hall, situated on a rocky outcrop overlooking the Stour Valley was the manor house of Gilbert le Dunsley. The present building, pictured in 1918, still contains some of the original building's timbers. In 1812, its then owner, Benjamin Robins, was murdered by a travelling carpenter who was subsequently traced, arrested, tried and executed at Stafford. His body was brought back to the scene of the crime, a local wood, and 'gibbeted' – placed in an iron cage – and hung from a tree for twelve months. Not surprisingly the area became known as Gibbet Wood, and the track to Stourbridge Gibbet Lane.

STOURTON CASTLE. FRONT ENTRANCE DRIVE.

Opposite: Stourton Castle began life as a Royal Hunting Lodge probably in the 11th century when it is reputed that King William II was in Kinver. Since then it has had links with a number of kings and their courts, namely Henry II, John, Edward IV, Henry VII and Henry VIII. Cardinal Pole was born at the castle in 1500, but after falling out of favour with Henry VIII spent some time abroad. On one occasion it was reported that he declined the election as Pope. As Archbishop of Canterbury, says Arthur Mee (*The King's England – Staffordshire*), Pole was implicated in 'religious persecutions of violence and horror' during Queen Mary's reign.

During the Civil War Stourton appeared to adopt a neutral role, but after the Cromwellians took it over Royalist forces from Worcester routed the Cromwellians at Stourbridge Heath and claimed the castle for the King. After a chequered career in turbulent times, the castle was then occupied by tenants and owners who were all either pioneers in the iron-working industry which sprang up in the Stour Valley or, in later years, were leaders in the industrial and commercial life of the Black Country. Today the castle remains in private hands. The best view of the castle and its gardens is from the towpath of the Staffordshire & Worcestershire Canal.

Dunsley House was built in the early 1800s and, as 'Dunsley Villa', was occupied by the Hancox family until the mid-1860s. It was used as a rest home by the Girls' Friendly Society from 1912 until the 1930s.

Rockmount, Dark Lane, was the birthplace of Kinver's most famous daughter, actress and author Nancy Price. It was built in or before 1624; in 1672 it became known as The Stone House and, in the 1860s, Rockmount. In her autobiography *Into an Hour Glass*, Nancy tells of the ghost of a former vicar of Kinver the Revd John Newley, that haunted the house. What the vicar's connections were with the house have never been recorded.

Opposite: Nancy Price was born in Kinver in 1880. Her father, William Henry Price and her grandfather ran a prosperous canal haulage company in Brierley Hill and played a major part in forming what was to become one of the largest canal carrying fleets in England – Fellows, Morton & Clayton Ltd. From an early age she was destined for an illustrious stage career and became widely regarded as one of England's finest character actresses. Despite her success on the London stage, she never lost her affection for Kinver. In addition to her stage career as an actress and eventually a producer, she wrote several books and in one she wrote: 'Almost every sixth dream is about Kinver, my old home and the Church there.' In 1950 she was awarded the CBE for her services to the theatre. She died in 1970, aged ninety.

Nancy Price's wedding in 1907 was probably the social event of the year for Kinver with the reception being held literally on two levels in the magnificent gardens of the family home. In the upper garden, family and personal friends were seated at individual tables and in this picture several have been identified. The bride and bridegroom, Mr Charles Maude, are pictured on the right. Seated (second left) is Mr Cole, the Grammar School headmaster and behind him is Mr Raglan Neale, the proprietor of the White Harte Hotel. To Mr Cole's immediate left is Mrs Alice Bills and Mr Albert James Bills, village chemist, and seated (extreme right) is Miss Dorothy Bills.

Old Grammar School House was the village's grammar school from the late 1550s until it closed down through lack of money and pupils in around 1913. The school's origins can be traced back to 1511 when the local priest was instructed to 'teach Grammar to Kinver children'. Whilst the date of founding is unknown, it was one of many Chantry schools closed down by Edward VI. When the King later granted a number of charters for grammar schools, Kinver was not included; the nearest was King Edward VI School, Stourbridge. Local people then raised sufficient money to found the village's own grammar school and it continued successfully for around 350 years.

Opposite: In the lower garden and seated at a long table were Mr Price's employees and their partners who had presumably made the journey to Kinver on the Light Railway. The uniformed bandsmen are thought to have come from Stourbridge.

Formerly Hyde House, this 17th-century building was first owned by the Foley family of Hyde Iron Works and retained connections with the local iron industry until 1880. In 1906 the Revd E.G. Hexall, supported by voluntary contributions, renamed the house 'Bethany' and used it as a home where crippled children, some abandoned as babies by their parents, were educated and taught a trade within their physical capabilities. In seven years the home was caring for and training forty physically handicapped boys. It closed in about 1918 and a few years later the building was demolished. No trace of it remains.

CHAPTER EIGHT

THE VILLAGE FRINGE

Although the High Street was, and still is, at the heart of the village, on its outskirts are many features which, individually and collectively, have given Kinver its unique character.

As will be seen in the following pictures, open farmland that once stretched up to Kinver Edge has been built over, most of the development having taken place after 1950. This development was in response to the number of people wishing to move out of the West Midlands conurbation and live in a country area yet remain within easy reach of employment.

Periodically, developers attempt to spread outwards but the designated green belt surrounding the village, if retained, will ensure that Kinver remains at about its present size and will not suffer the fate of so many other Midland villages, which have become dormitory areas for the larger towns.

Now a private residence called Clifford Cottage, the workhouse on Church Hill was the second such establishment in Kinver. The first one was recorded in 1739 when three cottages in Swan Lane, later Vicarage Drive, were leased to the parish for twenty-one years and converted into a workhouse. By 1830 the workhouse had moved to Church Hill.

At the rear and to the side of Clifford Cottage was the old prison, the bulk of which had been excavated from the sandstone cliff and faced with brick as shown in this 1905 view.

Approaching the village down Dunsley Road was to travel down a country lane through open countryside. At the bottom of the hill can be seen the Vine Inn with Church Hill in the background. This photograph dates from about 1930.

Looking down The Holloway, a narrow track hewn out of sandstone between Church Hill and Mill Lane, c. 1920. At the top of The Holloway was the Catholic church, once a former school. The church closed in the 1980s.

Church Hill at its junction with Cookley Lane, *c.* 1915.

The same junction, this time looking towards Cookley, with a motorcycle combination heralding the forthcoming invasion of motor transport, *c.* 1920.

Foster Street (named after James Foster, a Stourbridge iron master and tenant of Stourton Castle) as seen in about 1926 from the playground of the former junior school in Enville Road, with Kinver Edge dominating the skyline. The houses were built and funded by an earlier Friendly Society in about 1850.

Potter's Cross and the 'Doll's Houses', so named because of their external appearance, in 1918. The fields to the right are now occupied by a number of shops, as seen below in 1950. The open fields in the background (right) are colonized by a large housing development built in the 1960s.

Viewed from Potter's Cross today, all the farmland seen bordering Meddins Lane in this 1916 postcard view has been covered with housing. Kinver Edge, mainly because it was used for grazing, carried very few trees. The four villas, including the shop, are still in existence as is the building (right background) which, for many years, was a small general store known as 'Ison's; much of its custom, including afternoon teas, came from day trippers.

The building of Council houses in 1930 marked the beginning of widespread housing development in the Potter's Cross, Meddins Lane and White Hill areas.

Enville Road from Potter's Cross, *c.* 1950, is not vastly different from today's street scene.

Hyde Lane looking towards Enville Road, *c.* 1950. The Edge in the background shows an increase in tree cover from that seen in earlier photographs.

Heathlands (Enville Road) looking towards Enville in 1917 – a scene that has changed little in 100 years.

This is another picture on which the Historical Society would like more information. Before the war, fairs regularly visited Kinver and one site was in what is now Fairfield Drive. The location of this one is not known.

Since the early part of this century Kinver has been a popular area for Scout and Guide activities. The pine woods which surround the Compa campsite are an ideal woodcraft training area, as seen in this 1913 photograph of a Scoutmaster and his young charges.

The Log Cabin was built in 1933 and opened on 3 June of that year by Lady Baden Powell. The entrance to the campsite was 'guarded' by the two totem poles shown below. Those pictured have been replaced. The site was provided by the Webb family for use by the Worcestershire Scout Association at a peppercorn rent and was sold to the Association in 1994.

Kinver was also a popular camping area for the Boys' Brigade, seen here on parade passing the Elizabethan House in High Street. The date of this event is unknown. The house has been undergoing restoration by the West Midlands Historic Buildings Trust and in 1996 received financial assistance from the National Lottery.

Kinver has always been a lively community ready to celebrate any event of national or local importance; one such enthusiastic organization was the 'Kinver Jubilee Jazzers'. This picture could have been for the 1935 Jubilee but any information would be welcomed by Kinver Historical Society.

CHAPTER NINE

TOURISM

T he unspoilt countryside, woodland and the open heathland of Kinver Edge has been a magnet for visitors from the Black Country for over a century. In the earliest days of Kinver as a tourism attraction, visitors were usually those fortunate enough to have their own horse and carriage or able to afford the relatively high cost of hiring a horse 'brake'.

When the Light Railway opened, Kinver experienced instant success as a day or half-day destination. By the time the railway closed in 1930, Kinver had a regular bus service to Stourbridge and coach operators had found Kinver a popular venue.

Today Kinver remains a favourite place among West Midlanders even though the motor car and motorways enable families to travel further afield for a day out. Happily Kinver has escaped much of the brash and intrusive commercialization that has ruined many other rural destinations.

MUSEUM COTTAGES, KINVER

Copyright L.Ltd.

KVR. 19

Winding up from the village towards Kinver Edge, the tourism 'trail' was well established by 1910. This postcard scene is of Museum Cottages in The Compa and their tea garden and shelter, *c.* 1920.

Opposite: Adjoining the cottage and tea garden was the Rock House Museum. This former sandstone dwelling was run by the owner, Mr Fairbridge (pictured with his cat), for some twenty years complete with a selection of the forerunners of today's one-armed bandits.

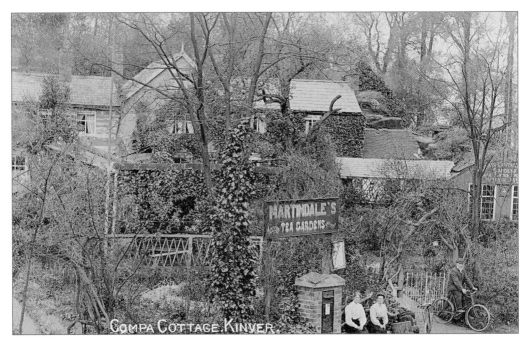

Nearby was another tourism enterprise, Martindale's Tea Rooms and Gardens. On the extreme right can be seen a large tea room sign which also advertised overnight accommodation for members of the Cyclists Touring Club.

The Compa and road junction looking from Church Hill, *c.* 1910. To the left is the road leading up to Edge View Hotel, Tea Rooms and Kinver Edge. To the right, a public footpath still leads to what is now Fairfield Drive. It was a well-trodden route used by the multitude of visitors going to and from the village centre and the Light Railway terminus. In the foreground is one of several groups of gaming machines so popular in cafés at that time.

Without doubt the largest single commercial enterprise in the village in the early part of the century was the Edge View Hotel in the Compa. In this scene, *c.* 1906, it was well patronized by day-trippers as well as residents. To the right can be seen the hotel's Café Royale tea room with seating for over 300 people. The enterprise eventually went bankrupt, its failure being blamed on the refusal of the local Licensing Justices to allow it to sell alcohol! It then became a sanatorium (linked to Prestwood Sanitorium) for the treatment of tuberculosis; it was said that the air around the surrounding pine woods contained healing properties for chest complaints. After several years and the virtual eradication of tuberculosis, it was used as a recovery and convalescence home. Another change of use saw it converted into a home for mentally handicapped people. It was closed down the 1970s but has now reopened as a residential care home.

The former Edge View Hotel as a tuberculosis hospital in 1920.

After the failure of the Edge View Hotel, the Wells family opened tea rooms on what is now Fairfield Drive, off Stone Lane. Adjoining ground, now occupied by Foley Infants' School, soon became a well-used coach park as can be seen from this picture of people making their way back to the tea rooms and coaches, *c.* 1930. Several of the coaches pictured are believed to have been operated by Samuel Johnson 'Supreme' of Stourbridge, with others, including the one in the centre with a white roof, operated by Midland Red probably from the company's Foster Street garage in Stourbridge.

As Kinver grew in popularity among day-trippers, there were also many who bought small plots of land nearer Kinver Edge and the woodland and built small chalets or cottages as holiday homes. This photograph, *c.* 1918, shows a number of such chalets and cottages in the area now occupied by Church View Gardens, Compton Gardens and Compton Road. Needless to say, such development was before Town and Country Planning legislation had been enacted.

Sandy Lane, leading from the top of Kinver Edge and the National Trust Warden's cottage to Blakeshall, is now a heavily-used road particularly on summer weekends and is a far cry from this early 1920s scene, when it was what its name suggested.

The wide open space of Kinver Edge and the 'Eleven Apostles' – a clump of trees – as seen in about 1920. The 'Roman Encampment' referred to on the postcard is, in fact, the earthwork ramparts of an Iron Age Fort which in recent years have been cleared of scrub to reveal the extent of the fortification ditches.

CHAPTER TEN

ROCK HOUSES

A major attraction to Kinver for generations has been its cluster of Rock Houses. The earliest record of habitation was in 1814 when the burial was recorded of a woman, aged seventy-four, who had lived there. In 1914 there were about fourteen families living in the Rock Houses but by the 1950s all the families had been rehoused, although one house continued to be used as a café until 1967.

The frequently held view that the Rock Houses had been developed from prehistoric caves has never been proven. Certainly the dwellings nearest the village were on the site of an old sandstone quarry, which fell into disuse when it was found the sandstone was too soft to be of use in construction work. However, it was easy to fashion into living rooms which were warm in winter and cool in summer.

While many of the remains of the Rock Houses in the Kinver area now lie on private land, a group of them are now in National Trust ownership. The Trust has restored one group as an exact copy of the original houses; local Trust volunteers cleared a substantial area of scrubland and returned it to the type of cultivation which existed at the turn of the century.

This postcard view, *c.* 1908, shows Mrs Charlotte Shaw in the garden of one of the 'top level' rock houses, with the stone and tile extensions hiding other rooms carved out of the sandstone.

A view of the Holy Austin rock houses and gardens as seen from Compton Road, *c.* 1903.

On the 'bottom level', *c.* 1910. This house was lived in by Mr and Mrs Fletcher in 1900, and they are featured in a painting by Alfred Rushton which now hangs in the Constitutional Club, Kinver.

Another resident of one of the 'bottom level' rock houses, *c.* 1915. The only major change from the picture above is the renewed wooden frame at the well-head.

Also on the bottom level and facing Stone Lane and Compton Road, this rock house, *c.* 1910, had the unusual feature of the living-room chimney brickwork following the contour of the cliff face. This house was the setting of the 1919 film 'Bladys of the Stewponey', which was financed by a Kinver man and Black Country industrialist, Benjamin Priest.

Mrs Martindale making lace at her rock house home, *c.* 1910.

Nanny's Rock, *c.* 1928. There is no evidence that this was ever used as a dwelling in the accepted sense of the word, for in its five chambers there is no sign of door or window frames having been installed. However, one of the caves was known as 'Mag-o'-Fox' hole, *c.* 1680, a name which may have been derived from the name of a woman 'Margaret of the Fox Earth' who was said to have lived there and whose death was recorded in 1617. When this photograph was taken, generations of sightseers had carved their initials in the sandstone.

A general view of Nanny's Rock, *c.* 1914. How the outcrop gained this name has never been satisfactorily explained, unless one of the caves may have been used centuries ago by a hermit. This suggestion, like many others, may be based purely on supposition or just pure romanticism. . . .

HERE & THERE: A MISCELLANY OF THE VILLAGE COMMUNITY

Unlike many communities, Kinver has managed to retain its own identity and in many ways has developed a highly distinctive and independent image. It can be argued that it has more social, occupational and sporting activities than many other communities of similar or even larger size.

Although retaining its basically rural character, the community has successfully kept pace with developments in the modern lifestyle, without becoming a commuter overspill satellite of the West Midlands conurbation.

The village has a tradition of good educational facilities which date back to over 400 years ago, when the inhabitants financed their own grammar school. Although that school has now closed, others have continued to flourish.

Today, there are at least seventy individual organizations in the village including activities as varied as drama, local history studies, horticulture, music, wine-making, cricket, football and model engineering. Examples in the following pages of this collective and individual energy going back nearly a century are, in themselves, proof of a successful self-contained rural community, which few want to leave and many want to join.

Above: This picture of Kingsford Lane, *c.* 1908, is reminiscent of a Constable painting and is a far cry from today's Kingsford Lane. Although the area is heavily wooded there are now numerous car-parks and picnic areas forming part of the Kingsford Country Park.

On the other side of Kinver Edge from Kingsford Lane is Blakeshall Lane, pictured here in 1910. One family enjoys the 'freedom' of the motor car.

Management, staff and VIPs line up for the photographer in 1908 at the opening of the Mill Lane Waterworks, from an original photograph in the Kinver Historical Society archives. The site is now occupied by Mill House.

Pipe laying in The Holloway, *c*. 1910.

Below: Sewerage pipes being laid at The Compa in the 1920s, reflecting the expansion of development away from the village centre. The Martindale and other tea rooms can be seen in the background.

A traction engine hauling timber in Kinver early this century (date unknown). The engine, according to a sign on its boiler, belonged to an Amblecote haulage contractor.

Steam power on the farm. A stationary steam engine at work driving a threshing machine during harvest time on a Kinver farm. Although no date is known, it could have been in the 1890s as the engine itself was horse drawn.

A local farmer, Mr S. Piper, proudly displays his prize certificate awarded for his cow, *c.* 1911.

The largest fox ever killed in Britain and recorded in the *Guinness Book of Records* was this one shot at Lydiatts Coppice, Greyfields Estate, on 11 March 1956. It weighed 28 lbs 2 oz, was 54 inches long from nose to tail and stood 21 inches high at the shoulder.

Kinver fire engine outside the George and Dragon, High Street whilst taking part in the 1936 Silver Jubilee celebration parade. At one time the village's chemist, Mr Frank Bills, was the local brigade's chief officer.

With the outbreak of the Second World War this Lanchester saloon car was converted into a fire tender. The rear panels were cut away and seating installed for the crew. It pulled a trailer on which was loaded a high capacity water pump. Although also used to fight local fires, it was, happily, never called on to fight the effects of enemy action in the village. The cost of conversion was met by money left over from the village's 1937 Coronation Fund.

Kinver Boys' Council School sports prizewinners, *c.* 1910, and (below) another group of sports winners from the same school in 1912.

A group of pupils from Kinver Boys' Council School with their Headmaster Mr A.L. Shepherd, *c.* 1912.

Group 2 from Kinver Infants' School with their teacher, Miss Angel, *c.* 1910.

The whole of the Boys' Council School assembled for this picture in 1913.

Opposite: The day the FA Cup came to Kinver in 1954. Through the good offices of former West Bromich Albion star Arthur Fitton, who later became Kinver's National Trust warden, the village had a sight of that famous trophy. It was won by 'The Baggies' with a 3–2 victory over Preston North End on 1 May of that year.

Kinver Football Club with the Kidderminster Junior Cup which they won in the 1948/49 season with a 2–1 victory over Barnsley Sports at Victoria Park, Quarry Bank. Back row, left to right: Bill Taylor, George Hadley, Jack Lane, John Wickens, 'Taxi' Timmins, Bob Glover, Tony Jordan. Front row: Reg Saunders, 'Dabber' Davies, Harold Price (captain), Norman Collins and Ken Saunders.

A dinner of the Royal Antedeluvian Order of Buffaloes at the Green Dragon (later the Constitutional Club), *c.* 1917. What the event was is not recorded.

A children's 'street party' at the rear of the Old Plough celebrates the 1953 Coronation.

The Kinver tourist trade of the early 20th century made maximum use of the seaside-style of comic postcards for visitors to send to relatives and friends. Some were of the typical 'wish-you-were-here' style while others were, for those days, somewhat 'saucy'. Here are two examples of the more 'respectable' ones.

'Business as usual' (facing page, above and overleaf). In the darkest days of the Second World War, September 1941, Kinver village businesses did their best to appear as if nothing had changed, as can be seen from these advertisements which appeared in the Parish Church magazine.

CHAPTER TWELVE

ENVILLE

Enville village is one of the few villages remaining close to the West Midlands conurbation that has escaped the spread of suburbia. This is due, no doubt, to the surrounding green belt. Much of the area is within the Enville Hall estate and the village lies within a conservation area.

The village has remained a closely knit community over the centuries. The parish as a whole comprises a number of isolated farmhouses and cottages which reflect their origins within the Kinver Forest.

Totally rural, Enville parish once comprised three manors – the Anglo-Saxon settlements of Enville and Morfe – with Lutley being first mentioned in the 12th century.

Straddling the Stourbridge–Bridgnorth road, the village centre lies at the foot of a ridge on the summit of which stands the parish church.

Adjoining the village is Enville Hall which has remained in the same family for over 400 years. In the Hall grounds is the cricket field; laid in 1821 it was regarded at the time as superior to Lord's. The first match was played in 1821 and has been played there ever since.

Enville parish church as seen today is the result of a substantial restoration by Sir Gilbert Scott between 1872 and 1874, when substantial internal and external work was carried out including the reconstruction of the tower. Standing on a ridge alongside the Bridgnorth Road, the church occupies a dominant position above the village and although there is no record of when the first church was built, architectural evidence indicates the existence of a church on this site by the 12th century. The Church of St Mary was an invocation in use by the 18th century although in the 16th century the name St Laurence was in use. Earlier, in the Middle Ages, there was an altar dedicated to St Nicholas. Nonconformity flourished for only a short time in the village. In 1855 a house in the village was opened for use by the Wesleyan Methodists, but about two years later the meetings were abandoned because of opposition by the Rector, Cornelius Jesson.

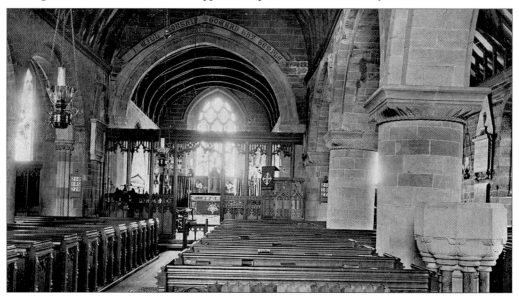

A view of Enville village from the parish church, looking towards Kinver.

The picturesque approach to Enville along the Stourbridge road as seen here, about seventy years ago, has hardly changed today apart from a wider carriageway.

Stamford House was built in 1857 as the Stamford Arms Hotel to cater for visitors to the Hall gardens and cricket festivals. It closed in 1892 when the gardens were no longer open to the public and it became a private residence. It was demolished in 1950.

The village war memorial was erected on a triangular piece of land (see previous picture) adjoining the road to the Hall. This photograph may have been taken at the memorial's dedication, date unknown.

Enville Village with Blundies Lane to the left, *c.* 1905. Beyond the buildings (which included a shop) stood the village school, which was opposite the Cat Inn.

Looking towards Bridgnorth, the parish church tower can be seen on the ridge overlooking the village.

The Cat Inn, *c.* 1903. First mentioned in 1777, this was one of two inns in that period, the other being the Swan Inn. Another inn, The Crown, was known to exist in 1642 but there is a suggestion that it may have existed as early as 1582. Still a popular hostelry, The Cat Inn is unusual in that it only retains a six day licence. It never opens on a Sunday.

Avenue, Enville Hall   Valentines Series

Enville Hall is the predominant feature of the village, the economic welfare of which was almost totally dependent on the Hall and its vast estate. Before the conquest, the manor was held by Alric, a King's thegn. The manor passed through several hands until, in 1528, Lord Dudley sold it to Sir Edward Grey of Whittington, Kinver, whose descendants still own it. No trace of the original manor house remains. It was replaced in around 1548 by a new house built by Grey. Over the ensuing 400 years, the Hall has had many additions and its gardens, of some 60 acres, were described in the 1880s as some of the finest in the country. The Hall eventually became the home of the Earl of Stamford and Warrington. The title became extinct in 1883 with the death of the seventh Earl and ownership was passed down through the female line. Pictured below is the tree-lined drive to the Hall from the Kinver Road, the main entrance being from the village centre.

The north front of Enville Hall, pictured after restoration following a fire in 1904.

The south front and entrance.

The remarkable and ornate conservatory which housed specimen exotic plants from around the world was built in 1855 and was described as being 'second only to Crystal Palace' for sheer size and magnificence. It was demolished in 1927. Extraordinary though the Conservatory was, the Hall's gardens, lakes and much of the parkland attracted thousands of visitors each summer in the 1860s in their own right. At one time the gardens and parkland were so large that a staff of over thirty was employed to manage it. The first major work done on landscaping the area was by the poet and landscape designer, William Shenstone of The Leasowes, Halesowen, whose work was commemorated by Shenstone's Chapel on the edge of woodland. Later further landscaping was carried out, and so large was the area that a carriage road was built to enable visitors to travel through it.

The Sea Horse Pool, *c.* 1905. There were many fish ponds, ornamental lakes and fountains in the gardens, the fountains being gravity-fed from a four million gallon reservoir to which water was supplied through two steam-powered pumps.

A group of Hall staff, *c.* 1914. Standing, left to right: Walter Broughton (plumber), Charlie Howard (Hall/kitchen) Bert Lickett (chauffeur – presumably on Army leave). Seated: George Wood and Frank Bowen (chauffeurs).

Chauffeur Frank Bowen (above) with the family's Studebaker and (below) Sam Weaver, occupation unknown, with the Daimler.

Without doubt the biggest disaster to befall Enville Hall was the fire on 25 November 1904 which gutted much of the central part of the building. In this photograph, taken some twenty-four hours after the outbreak, can be seen one of two steam-powered horse-drawn pumps which had made a perilous 5 mile dash from Stourbridge through snow and on icebound roads. A graphic description of the fire and the frantic efforts of the Hall and Estate employees to save many of the buildings' treasures appeared in the *County Express*. The detailed report described the perilous cycle ride of a Hall employee made on snow and icebound roads to alert the Stourbridge Fire Brigade nearly 6 miles away. Hauling a heavy 'steamer' fire engine, the team of horses had several falls in the treacherous conditions before arriving at the Hall at 3.40 am. At 5.00 am, a second 'steamer' arrived from Stourbridge. Together with the Hall's own manual pump, which frequently froze up, the two engines pumped about 1,000 gallons of water an hour from the nearby Sea Horse Pool for nearly twenty-four hours.

While staff struggled to save valuable works of art from the stricken centre of the building, the firemen battled to keep the fire away from the ballroom and the library, which housed 'masterpieces of art and rare editions'. Once contained, the fire 'continued to burn for three days and smouldered for two weeks'. Throughout the whole episode, the Hall's fire brigade remained diligently on duty. The cause of the fire was never precisely established but was thought to have spread from a chimney fire in one of the guest bedrooms which was being prepared for a shooting and house party the following day.

Aware of the Hall's isolated position, Lord Stamford founded the Enville Hall Household Fire Brigade in the 1820s. Pictured is the same manual twelve-man pump built in 1826 which unsuccessfully tried to bring the blaze under control pending the arrival of the Stourbridge steam pumps. The old manual pump was restored by Kinver firemen.

Rebuilding work in progress on the central part of the Hall which was completely gutted. Remarkably the family's gold and silver plate which was stored in a strong room at the centre of the blaze was undamaged.

Enville Hall was also the centre of much field sport activity and had its own racecourse, the Harkaway Point-to-Point course. Standing by one of the fences are (left) John Braithwaite of Blundies Farm and (right) William Shepherd, parish church verger and sexton.

This picture, *c.* 1903, remains a mystery. Was it a gamekeeper's cottage? And where was it situated?

A Hunt Meet outside the Cat Inn. The date is unknown.

In 1950 Lord Cobham of Hagley Hall (seated second right) and the MCC President brought E.R.T. Holmes's XI in to play a centenary match against Enville Cricket Club. Those pictured (left to right, back row) are: Merritt, Maxwell, Chesterton, Morkell, Watts, Carr. Seated are Seller, Allen, Holmes, Cobham, Howarth. The Enville team is pictured overleaf.

The Enville team playing the E.R.T. Holmes's XI was no less than eighteen strong and the game ended in a draw. In this pre-match photograph are (left to right); front row: Shaw, Leadbetter, Bourne, Bissell, Parkes, Higginson, Hodges. Middle row: Ward-Booth (Rector of Enville), Oakley, Vaughan, Jordan, Taylor, Fletcher, Adams, Perry, Humphries, Major Vaughan. Back row: guest, C. Shaw, Bullock, Smith, H. Shaw, Fitton.

ACKNOWLEDGEMENTS

The authors gratefully acknowledge the assistance of Mr David Bills, President of Kinver Historical Society, for his unlimited patience in double-checking the numerous historical facts that emerged in the production of the text accompanying the photographs and for the use of vintage photographs from his own private collection. Acknowledgement is also made of the Historical Society's generosity in allowing access to their archives and Mrs Val Hampton for providing details of Miss Nancy Price. In return, the authors are happy to ask readers to contact the Historical Society should they have any village archive material they may wish to donate.

KINVER & ENVILLE: A SECOND SELECTION

Like all holiday haunts, Kinver had a selection of 'comic' cards. This is a favourite from early in the twentieth century.

INTRODUCTION

Having existed for over 1,200 years in various forms and with various names, Kinver has become arguably one of the best known and most popular villages of South Staffordshire and North Worcestershire – a popularity that can be traced back well over a hundred years – and has become an integral part of the Black Country heritage, even though the village has never been a physical part of that area.

Kinver first made an appearance in AD 736 as 'Cynibre', a name relating to a woodland. Then in 964 the area was known as 'Cynfare' (a royal road) and in the Domesday Book of 1086 as 'Chenevare' (a great ridge or edge), king's land in which there were two mills and a manor.

Although Kinver had a thriving ironworking industry powered by mills on the River Stour as far back as the seventeenth century, the lack of local coal prevented any expansion; Kinver's iron industry was eventually eclipsed by the booming Black Country and its 'dark, satanic mills'.

Even in the nineteenth century the attraction of Kinver was well known. The well-to-do families of the Black Country came by horse-drawn coach and many built properties in and around the village – some as permanent homes, others as weekend and holiday retreats.

The arrival of James Brindley's Staffordshire & Worcestershire Canal brought some economic benefits. Apart from being a reliable and cheaper form of transport for goods it also meant cheaper coal as well as providing a number of jobs on the wharves.

During the late nineteenth century hundreds of miles of steam and then electrically powered tramways were laid throughout the Black Country and Birmingham, and in 1901 the Kinver Light Railway (which ran between Amblecote and Kinver) was opened. The 'Kinver Trams' as they were popularly known were an immediate success, and so Kinver was catapulted into the tourist industry in no small way.

Apart from bringing heavy seasonal tourist traffic, the trams marked Kinver's first steps towards becoming a 'commuter village'. Cheap and reliable transport meant people could return home to the clean air of Kinver after a day's work in the grime and smoke of the Black Country. The arrival of the private motor car and of buses and coaches (or charabancs) led to a decline in tramway traffic, with the line eventually closing in 1930.

Even during the Second World War, when private motoring was banned, visitors crowded on to the normal service buses from Stourbridge for a day out in the Kinver countryside.

Surprisingly the advent of motorways, package holidays, safari parks and theme parks has had no serious effect on Kinver's appeal. The draconian hand of development has largely passed it by and as so much of its centre has remained much as it did a hundred years ago perhaps that is its enduring appeal.

This publication, as a companion to the earlier volume published in 1996, contains many rare postcards plus private photographs never before published, and thus captures something of the mystique of a unique English village.

A postcard showing views of Kinver in the early twentieth century. Visitors from all over Britain must have sent copies home to their families.

STAFFORDSHIRE & WORCESTERSHIRE CANAL

The Staffordshire & Worcestershire Canal was the first link to be completed in James Brindley's ultimate plan for creating a 'Grand Cross' of canals to link the Thames, Severn, Trent and Mersey rivers and their ports. When completed in 1772 it was 46 miles long between its junction with the Trent & Mersey Canal at Great Haywood, near Stafford, and the River Severn at what was to become Stourport. The completion of the canal can thus be regarded as marking the start of the canal building era, which reached a peak in 1793 with over 2,000 miles of inland waterways in operation.

The section between Wolverhampton and Stourport was opened in November 1770 which meant that boats would have begun appearing in Kinver in late 1769.

When the Stourbridge Canal arrived at Stourton Junction (near the Stewponey) on 3 December 1779, Stourton became one of the busiest junctions on the English canal system as raw materials and goods to and from the Black Country passed through.

Although the arrival of railways led to a slow decline in canal traffic (with many railway companies absorbing the canals) the Staffordshire & Worcestershire, together with the Stourbridge Canal, retained their independence right up to nationalisation in 1948; indeed, one of the last acts of the Staffordshire & Worcestershire Canal Company was to pay a final dividend to its shareholders.

With the sudden cessation of coal traffic to Stourport Power Station in 1948 commercial traffic virtually ended. The canal's condition rapidly deteriorated and by the mid-1950s it was being considered for closure. Fortunately the presence of a boat building and holiday hire cruiser firm, Dawncraft, at Kinver and another hire cruiser base at Stourport, together with a lively public campaign against closure being waged by the newly formed Staffordshire & Worcestershire Canal society, ensured the canal's survival.

By the 1970s a new canal era had dawned – that of leisure cruising. Today in terms of traffic, the canal is said to be in the top three cruising stretches of water run by British Waterways. Kinver offers the most popular visitor moorings in its entire length. Between March and the end of October there are an estimated 9,000 boat movements through Kinver; many of these boats stop for up to forty-eight hours, and such visits make an important contribution to the village's tourism income.

Stewponey Wharf in its trading heyday nearly a hundred years ago with canal company employees, boatmen and local hauliers. To the left a boatman is about to 'draw the paddles' and fill the lock for the boat. On the wharf is a pile of salt with a cart also loaded with salt ready for local delivery; the salt could have come from either Droitwich (via the Worcester & Birmingham Canal or the River Severn) or from Nantwich, Cheshire. Also on the lockside is what was either coal slack or black ash from a Black Country foundry. The foundry ash was widely used as a cheap tow-path surfacing material: foundry owners were only too glad to give it away.

The two buildings in the background were canal company-owned and occupied by employees. The three-storey block (with an office on the ground floor) is thought to have been the home of the tall man on the lockside. Next to him is believed to be his father, Mr Moore. Mr Moore (junior) at nearly 7 ft tall was said to have a fearsome reputation as a bare knuckle boxer, with challenge fights being held on the lockside. Whether that is fact or romantic fiction is anyone's guess!

The entrance to the Staffordshire & Worcestershire Canal Company's wharf at Stewponey, *c.* 1930 – at roughly the time the tramlines were lifted but before the new road bridge was built. With the redesigning of the road junction for the new bridge, the entrance to the wharf was sealed off with access then being via the old bridge – an arrangement that still exists today. An AA patrolman is seen alongside a rather smart-looking sports car of that era. On the wharf, the Toll Office (left) remains – a listed building – as do the company cottages. The large building next to the Toll Office was later demolished.

Dunsley Tunnel (right) at 23 yards long is believed to be the oldest navigable canal tunnel in existence; it would have been built in about 1769 as the canal was built through Kinver and south to Stourport. There are only two tunnels on the canal, the other being at Cookley (65 yards long). Both were unusual for their time as they included tow-paths; normally boat horses would be led over the hill along a company 'horse road'.

The canal has always been noted for good fishing. The scene above, *c.* 1900, is on the approach to Dunsley Tunnel and is not much different today. The wooden barrier in the foreground allowed the boat tow lines to travel over the entrance into a culvert leading to a flood relief valve seen on the right. At times of exceptional rainfall there was always the danger of the canal breaching its bank; here the valve would be opened to allow surplus water to run off into the nearby River Stour. The picture (left) is taken from roughly the same spot looking towards Stewponey.

Two views of Hyde Lock, Kinver. Above, this postcard view was taken looking towards Kinver Edge, *c.* 1920. The lock has its top gate open, which would indicate an approaching boat. The card was specially commissioned for Kinver newsagents Jennings. Below is a scene taken some years later looking towards The Hyde bridleway bridge. The house in the distance was built for the Hyde Iron Works, and is all that is left of what was once Kinver's largest employer – the first iron slitting mill in England.

A postcard scene looking away from Kinver Lock. Though undated, this scene is probably late 1930s. The motorboat (with a smart sun canopy) is moored to land owned by the Vine Inn; it was possibly used for canal trips. Trading boats were still working the canal, and a boatman and his horse are seen approaching.

A view from the canal bridge: on the tow-path side is the wharf edge and a gateway leads to the gas works. This picture could have been taken in about 1948 as trade appears to have dropped off: the wharf edge (left) was in disrepair and, beyond some private boats, a former working boat had apparently found new life as a residential boat.

When the canal was a busy commercial waterway, scenes like this at Kinver Lock were commonplace. Above, a Shropshire Union Railway boat *Stourport* is tied up at the wharf adjoining the Vine Inn. On the wharf are piles of building bricks. These boats were owned by the Shropshire Union Canal Company which had been taken over by what was to become the LMS railway. They regularly travelled through Kinver on their way to the company's depots at Kidderminster and Stourport. The barrels seen on the boat could be empties being returned to a Stourport vinegar works, most of whose output was transported by canal. The picture below was taken much earlier and shows the LMS boat *Edris* fully 'sheeted-up' about to work down Kinver Lock.

Kinver's importance as a canal transport centre is further seen in this picture (date unknown). In the foreground is a hand-operated wharf crane while the lock cottage (minus the stairs to the loft) is unchanged even today. The building opposite the lock was a weighbridge office while on the opposite side of the road stood the Lock Inn. This pub was built shortly after the canal was fully opened with the bulk of its custom for alcohol and stabling coming from boatmen. It pre-dated the Vine Inn by many years – the latter was never built as a 'boatman's pub'.

A heavily laden coal boat heads away from Kinver. It was probably one of 'the light boats' – the boatman's name for the boats which carried coal to Stourport Power Station.

A tranquil scene, *c.* 1920, looking towards Gibraltar – a name given to an area dominated by sandstone cliffs which had been exposed when the canal was cut through in *c.* 1770. The name was certainly in existence in 1780. There were a number of rock houses hewn in the rock face, and even after they had been deemed unfit for habitation in 1880 a number continued to be used by boatmen and men working on the canal wharves.

Whittington Horse Bridge is said to have gained its name because it was built to carry a pack-horse trail over the canal. The pack-horse trail was believed to run from Stourbridge to the inland port of Bewdley; it was the arrival of the canal at Stourport which put Bewdley out of business. The trail then crossed the River Stour on what is still referred to as the Pack-Horse Bridge.

From Stourton Junction the Stourbridge Canal travels through relatively unspoilt countryside to Wordsley Junction, Stourbridge and Brierley Hill, where it meets the Dudley Canal. This scene is taken from New Town Bridge (Prestwood Drive) looking towards Wordsley. To the right was a row of Stourbridge Navigation Company cottages; it is now one private dwelling adjoining a narrowboat building yard. To the left and at several other points along the canal were a number of wharves serving sand quarries; almost all of the sand was destined for foundries and the building industry in the Black Country.

This final look at the canal will amuse canal enthusiasts and local historians. A comparatively modern (c. 1960) postcard shows Kinver lock in an unkempt state – other than for freshly painted lock gate balance beams. The unknown photographer obviously did not do his (or her) research very well and decided that the waterway was the 'Union Canal' and not the Staffordshire & Worcestershire Canal. Note that by this time the Lock Inn had been demolished and the Vine Inn was not yet a free house.

CHAPTER FOURTEEN

THE IRON ROAD

When the iron-working industry on the banks of the River Stour ended in the nineteenth century, unable to compete with the expanding Black Country industries with their ready and local supply of fuel and raw materials, Kinver's fortunes went into decline. There was a substantial fall in population as some families moved out to seek their fortunes in the Black Country. Many others emigrated overseas to new opportunities which were opening up in North America, Australia and New Zealand.

Kinver, however, still retained a special place in the minds of Black Country folk. Fresh country air, the scent of the pinewoods and the 'wide open spaces' offered a much-needed break, albeit for only a day, from the smoke-laden and congested industrial areas.

In the late nineteenth century only the more affluent could afford the cost of travel by horse-drawn 'brake' – or indeed their own horse-drawn transport. Nevertheless they formed the beginnings of the Kinver tourist industry, which developed in a truly spectacular fashion once the Kinver Light Railway was built and opened between Amblecote and the village. In the 1890s there had been a huge expansion of tramways throughout the neighbouring conurbation in the West Midlands and it was only a matter of time before Parliamentary approval was sought and given for a tramway to Kinver. In 1895 there was even a suggestion by the London Midland & Scottish Railway to built a branch line to Kinver!

On Good Friday, 5 April 1901, public services began. The company's hopes of running double-deck trams were thwarted by the Board of Trade, whose inspector ruled that the line's construction was simply not good enough for the heavier cars. Nevertheless the line experienced considerable success. Quite apart from its appeal to visitors, it heralded the start of the Kinver commuter, with villagers now able to work in the towns and still live in the country. The prosperity it brought to Kinver can be judged from this selection of photographs.

However, the arrival of regular bus and motor coach services from Stourbridge and further afield eventually saw the line close, in company with almost every other Black Country tramway, in 1930.

Much of the line's route between the village and the Stewponey can still be traced. At one time it was possible to walk much of the route, with all the bridges crossing the Stour still in place. Could it be that one day a tramway restoration society will be formed and the most scenic part of the line will be brought back into use as yet another tourist attraction?

The original tramway wooden bridge over the canal at Stewponey. In later years it was replaced by one of iron girder construction with enclosed sides. The tramway's publicity department took many photographs of the more scenic parts of line, particularly approaching The Hyde and Hyde Meadows. The picture below was a particular favourite.

Presumably these were the tramway publicists hard at work again, this time photographing a tram as it leaves the Stourton meadows to run alongside the canal as far as The Hyde.

One of the most popular and common of the many Kinver Light Railway postcards, picturing a Kinver-bound tram alongside the canal and approaching The Hyde. Even today at this point the track-bed of the tramway can be clearly seen – though the beech trees pictured are now some eighty years older.

Two more views of the tramway, only a few feet away from the canal. The location is more popularly known nowadays as 'The Beech Trees'.

One can appreciate that the tram ride to and from Amblecote must have been the high spot of any visit to Kinver. Certainly the company made the most of the scenery of Kinver and intensively marketed the area as 'The Switzerland of the Midlands'.

The tramway's main depot was at The Hyde, where a shed and several sidings were built on the site of the old ironworks. The huge mounds of slag which had been left when the works were demolished were used as track ballast between Kinver and Stewponey. Although there is no trace left of the shed in what is now dense woodland, the track-bed of the through line can still be seen. Below, Car 49 and its driver and conductor pose for yet another publicity photograph.

The end of the line at Kinver. Fortunately (as it turned out) the company made the Kinver terminus extremely spacious and capable of holding a large number of trams. Even so, on many Bank Holidays and summer weekends such was the volume of traffic, with cars coming from as far afield as West Bromwich and Birmingham, trams had to be parked at passing loops along The Hyde meadows prior to the homeward-bound rush.

A selection of different types of tramcar are lined up ready for the return journey from Kinver. At least three of the trams have been identified as from other tramways, and therefore must have been on special party charters.

This man was well known to the thousands of tourists who arrived by tram. Mr Sam Woodward was a conductor on the Kinver Light Railway and he is pictured outside his home in Church Hill. He later went on to live with his son in Woolaston where he died aged about 90.

CHAPTER FIFTEEN

MESSING ABOUT ON THE RIVER

Had it not been for a certain Andrew Yarranton running short of money and a freak storm over 300 years ago, the development of Kinver could have taken a different course. In 1667 Mr Yarranton had made the Stour navigable between Stourbridge and Kidderminster for the transport of coal, and it was his ambition to continue the navigation as far as the River Severn. His vision of a navigable link with the Severn was a century ahead of the great canal builder James Brindley's thinking, and he was spurred on by the promise of a fortune to be made. At this time Bewdley was a major inland port with goods being carried to and from the town by pack-horse trains, with at least one of the pack-horse trails travelling through Whittington – less than a mile from Kinver.

But at Kidderminster the Yarranton scheme stopped through lack of finance and when, in about 1670, a freak storm wrecked the whole of the navigation works, repairs could not be made and the navigation was abandoned.

Being a naturally fast-flowing river on its journey from Halesowen, the Stour had for centuries powered a large number of mills. The stretch of the river at Kinver was no exception with a mill weir close to the bridge. When tourists began to appear the enterprising mill owner opened a boating station; not only were rowing boats available for hire but he also ran a number of steam and motor launches. When the mill closed down and boating ended, the weir deteriorated and the river returned to its natural state.

There was a time when the Stour was a popular coarse-fishing river and there are records that for a while the tram operators ran early morning 'fishing specials' from Amblecote. However, as riverside industry expanded in Stourbridge, Lye and Halesowen, pollution increased and by the 1930s fish had disappeared. Forty years ago the Stour was regarded as one of England's most polluted rivers but more recently anti-pollution legislation has meant the river has steadily become cleaner, with some of its reaches once again supporting fish.

Eighty years ago the River Stour presented a very different picture from today. Because of a weir at Kinver, a considerable length of river was wide and deep enough for pleasure boating. The boating station at Kinver Mill was owned by Mr Timmings, who not only had a number of rowing boats for hire but actually ran trips on passenger boats; for a time he also operated a steam boat. The boating station and the mill were later owned by Mr Moses Clewes.

When the mill weir began to collapse and was eventually removed, the river immediately reverted to its natural state. Some years later the then Upper Stour Valley Main Sewerage Board deepened the river and piled up the dredging spoil on the banks to improve flood protection – and gave it today's appearance. From the late 1930s onwards the river became heavily polluted by industrial waste from riverside factories in Stourbridge, Lye and Halesowen and in the late 1940s the river ranked as one of the most polluted in England.

Kinver Bridge from just below the mill after widening and strengthening work had been completed. The houses to the right were eventually demolished, although The Stag public house remained for several years.

From time to time excessive rainfall caused the Stour to burst its banks. This was the scene in High Street in the early twentieth century.

CHAPTER SIXTEEN

INTO THE VILLAGE

The true English village, a self-contained community with its own special character moulded over centuries, is, according to many commentators, under threat if not from the seemingly relentless march of urban sprawl then certainly from the changing style of modern life. Over the years many villages have become residential areas of overspill from the towns with true village life and tradition being something almost alien to the newcomers. Out-of-town shopping areas and supermarkets have forced many traditional village general stores and post offices out of business and thus have removed an important part of village life. Equally many of a village's own clubs and societies have fallen by the wayside.

Kinver, however, is the exception. It has lost little of its original character and remains a thriving community. No doubt the natural and man-made barriers of a river, a canal and an arterial road have effectively separated it from the conurbation. The village's expansion has also been limited in parts by conservation area status, as well as by large areas of National Trust and countryside park and by a Green Belt policy so far rigidly enforced by local government. Kinver, therefore, is as well protected from modern pressures as any rural community can be.

These photographs cover over a hundred years and show that such changes that have occurred have not been too severe. In many respects today's village scene (apart from road traffic!) is not that much different from the days when Kinver was 'discovered' by the tourist.

It was evident as road traffic increased and buses arrived in Kinver that the old bridge had reached the end of its useful life. In 1921 it was widened and strengthened.

High Street from the bottom of Church
Hill and before the influx of tourists,
c. 1900. Even so these pictures show
there has been little major change in the
general appearance of High Street.

A few years later and the telegraph pole is proof of modern communications becoming part of village life. Tourism was also well under way as Mr Guttery was offering 'teas and apartments'. Even the pavements had been improved. The picture below was taken from outside The Cross public house (right) looking towards Mr Guttery's tea shop – which appears to have been newly whitewashed.

Vestiges of the original layout of the village can still be seen in this view from Church Hill. The long strips of land behind some of the properties are the remnants that date back to the time when Kinver was given a formal borough charter: a map of the 'borough' showed a similar layout of land. In 1798 the village was described as 'one long spacious street well paved with pebbles'.

The buildings adjoining the White Harte Hotel were demolished to make way for the 'Kinema Theatre'.

The coronation of King George V in 1910 was celebrated in traditional manner with a parade of village organisations along High Street. Enormous crowds were reported to have attended the celebrations, most of whom, no doubt, had come to Kinver by the tramway.

It would appear that these two pictures were also taken during coronation celebrations. Above, children from the Kinver National School stand near Vicarage Drive and in front of the school building in 1910. Below, residents of the Mill Lane cottages gather for a chat during the 1953 celebrations.

High Street in the early 1900s. In the distance are the almshouses. Below, the same location some twenty years later.

High Street, early 1900s. Judging from the appearance of what is now the Constitutional Club it had not long been built as a hotel on the site of the former Green Dragon public house, although the new building retained the old name.

Local children celebrate the coronation of Queen Elizabeth II with a street party in Mill Lane, and all proudly display their coronation mugs, 1953.

Two contrasting views of High Street. The postcard view (above) was commissioned by Miss J.E. Fletcher of Kinver post office. Judging by the number of pedestrians it could have been taken on a Saturday. Below, a quieter scene a few years later.

High Street, late 1920s. To the left is Ye Olde Green Dragon Hotel, still vainly hoping for
residential visitors. In 1936 it went out of business and became the Constitutional Club.

High Street, c. 1938. To the right is the imposing façade of the village pharmacy. In the same
building was the post office, which later moved to premises on the other side of the road.

Had they arrived . . . or were they just leaving? This early twentieth-century postcard shows two heavily laden horse-drawn 'brakes' outside the old Car and Horses public house in High Street. A note on the back of the photograph says it was a 'men only' outing. The word 'car' in the name of the pub was presumably short for 'carriage'.

This 1904 postcard was sent by a young man, Arthur Vivian, from Stourton Hall to a friend at Malvern. He must have had a vivid imagination for he refers to visiting 'caves where the Highway Robbers used to meet a long time ago'. And he must have been an honest lad, for the card also reads: 'I have only climbed two trees.'

At the far end of High Street, *c.* 1930 – and a group of small shops, one of which was known as 'Ye Olde Tobacco Shoppe' and also advertised its 'Kinver Rock'. Beyond is the Plough and Harrow public house. The row of cottages facing the camera were demolished in more recent times, with the site being transformed into Danesford Gardens – a public open space with seating.

Stone Lane, along which thousands of visitors trekked from the tram terminus on their way to Kinver Edge.

An early photograph of Stone Lane. To the left is Ye Olde Plough, which was demolished in 1997. The building to the right was part of a row of cottages which have been completely restored, although the corner shop remained until a few years ago. Stone Lane itself is virtually unrecognisable; the barn and cottage on the left were demolished to make way for Harris's (and then Lowe's) Garage. Fairfield Drive was built beyond the garage; along it was a large motor coach park and Wells's Tea Rooms.

The almshouses and other old cottages in High Street were some of the oldest properties in the road before they were demolished after being deemed unfit by the local authority, despite considerable local opposition. The demolition took place before much of the village had become a conservation area, and before there was such a thing as listed building status.

An early photograph of the National School for boys and girls which was built in 1851. A separate school for girls was built in 1873, and when new schools were built it eventually became the village library.

Old property in the process of demolition, next door to the new clinic and health centre.

The end of High Street, 1906. The buildings on the right were the Wesleyan Methodist Church and Sunday School. When the Methodist churches in Kinver amalgamated in a new church at Potters Cross, the old church and school hall were used as a youth club and a boxing club. But deterioration and vandalism eventually led to the site being cleared and the area being redeveloped for housing.

Overlooked by the original Kinver Boys' School is the Royal Exchange public house. For a time it was also known as The Cherry Tree. What is now parking space was a sitting-out area and veranda.

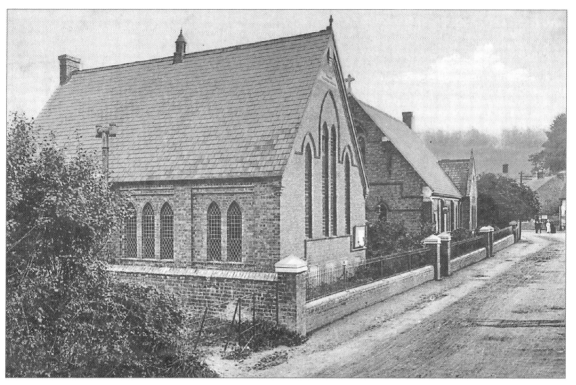

Kinver's two Methodist Churches: the Wesleyan Church in High Street above, and the Primitive Methodist Church at Potters Cross below. The second picture was taken shortly after the church building had been erected; the original corrugated-iron chapel (referred to by some as 'the tin chapel') can be seen in the background.

A striking photograph of the western end of the village from Kinver Edge, early 1950s. In the immediate foreground are the Rock Houses with 'TEAS' appearing in prominent white lettering on the rock face. The house built at right angles to the road was a general store known as Isons, which also did a roaring trade as tea gardens particularly during summer weekends. Beyond Meddins Lane can be seen the curve of a new road and a council housing development off White Hill. The large building in White Hill was the New Rose and Crown. In the centre background the large hilltop building is Hillboro House, owned by Cradley Heath industrialist Alf Ryland. The house was demolished in the 1960s and the land was used for high density housing.

At least twenty-five years separate these views of Potters Cross. Above, the Dolls' Houses with their mock-Tudor gables overlook the junction of Meddins Lane, Enville Road and White Hill. To the right is open farmland, which eventually became (below) a small shopping area. The top photograph was taken from Potters Farm, on which Brindley Heath Junior School was built in the 1970s.

Judging by the size of the trees, this photograph of the Dolls' Houses must have been taken only a few years after the property was built.

A postcard view of Meddins Lane where the first council houses in Kinver were built. The postcard was possibly produced for the builder, E.R. Tooby of Stourbridge.

A postcard view of Potters Cross, early 1900s. Running from left to right is Enville Road and directly ahead is White Hill. To the left is Meddins Lane. The large field was eventually developed for council housing.

White Hill was not much more than a country lane. The building to the right was the Cottage Spring public house. In later years it was replaced by the New Rose and Crown.

One of Kinver's best-known characters was Mr Archie Taylor, the village hairdresser whose main off-duty interest was conducting the Kinver Boys' Band. Stories are still told of customers sitting in the barber's chair suddenly being left for a few minutes, as Mr Taylor rushed into a back room where the band was practising to berate someone for blowing a wrong note! The picture below was probably one of the last taken of the band in action. Mr Taylor had marched them up to the top of Church Hill, and is here supervising a final rehearsal before the band appeared at a 1953 coronation celebration on Kinver Edge.

CHAPTER SEVENTEEN

PROMINENT PROPERTIES

For centuries Kinver has had many large and prestigious houses and several are still in existence. Although some began their lives as farmhouses others were built by prominent industrialists who saw in Kinver the ideal location – close enough to be in contact with their industrial empires but far enough away to avoid the smoke and pollution of the towns. The largest property in the parish is Stourton Castle.

This private photograph of Stourton Castle shows part of the immaculate gardens.

Stourton Castle (above) began life as a Royal Hunting Lodge probably in the eleventh century, when it is reputed that King William II visited Kinver. It had links with a number of kings and their courts and was the birthplace of Cardinal Pole. During the Civil War it was claimed by Royalists and the Roundheads. In more peaceful times it was then occupied by many tenants and owners, who were involved in the ironworking and engineering industries of first the Stour Valley and then the Black Country. The castle was the scene of many special events, one of which was the coming-of-age party of the ironmaster's son, William Henry Foster (below). This was attended by 2,000 employees of W.O. Foster MP, who saw the presentation of 'an Address' to the young Mr Foster.

Two prominent houses in the village were Redcliff (above) and Dunsley House (below). The latter was built in the early 1800s, and as Dunsley Villa was occupied by the Hancox family until the mid-1860s. From 1912 until the 1930s it was used as a rest home by the Girls' Friendly Society.

Stourton was a hamlet on the summit of the Bridgnorth Road and at its junction with Greensforge Lane. South Lodge (above) is an imposing property shielded from the main road by a high castellated wall. Over the years Stourton has also come to include the ribbon development of housing along the Bridgnorth Road from the parish boundary with Wollaston, Stourbridge. Pictured left are two unidentified gentlemen about to set off from South Lodge on a cycle ride.

A postcard view of Stourton post office, *c.* 1920.

One of a number of cottages built into the hillside on the Bridgnorth road, and looking across the field to The Hyde and Kinver.

An early photograph of the Old Grammar School House, probably taken shortly after it closed as a school. Its origins can be traced back to 1511 when the local priest was instructed to 'teach Grammar to Kinver children'. While the precise foundation date is unknown, the original institution was one of many chantry schools closed down during the Reformation. When King Edward VI granted a number of charters for grammar schools Kinver was not included, the nearest being King Edward VI School, Stourbridge. Local people raised sufficient money to re-establish the school, however, and it continued for 350 years. When the school closed most of its pupils transferred to King Edward's, Stourbridge.

The gardens of the School House.

A large seventeenth-century mansion, Hyde House was first owned by the Foley family of Hyde Iron Works and retained its links with the iron industry until 1880, when The Hyde works closed down. The picture above was taken before 1906, for in that year the Revd E.G. Hexall, supported by voluntary donations, occupied the building and renamed it Bethany. He used it as a home for crippled boys, most of whom had been abandoned by their parents. All the boys were taught a trade within their physical capabilities. At one time it was caring for and training forty boys. It closed in about 1918. A few years later the house was demolished – and no trace of it remains.

Mr Hexall must have been something of a hard-nosed publicist when it came to seeking financial support for the home. Visitors were always welcome and postcards such as this were widely distributed to tram passengers, urging them to alight at Hyde Meadows Halt and to visit Bethany.

When Mr Hexall died, it is said the whole of Kinver came to a standstill as the funeral cortège left the village. The funeral service was held at the Providence Chapel, Oldbury, and followed by interment at Spon Lane Cemetery. The funeral cortège was formed by two tramcars, between which was a wagon that had been converted into a bier. The cortège is pictured here passing through Wollaston.

CHAPTER EIGHTEEN

A VILLAGE MISCELLANY

While the traditional centre of Kinver – the High Street – is self evident, there is much more that makes up the whole picture. Together with the photographs which appeared in the first volume, this latest selection adds to understanding of the rich variety of a century of daily life within the village.

Regrettably few of the photographs we have uncovered give the names of the people or any information of the events portrayed; no doubt as the pictures are seen and discussed more details will emerge. The authors hope that such information will be gathered together and preserved for posterity.

The village from Church Hill. From Mill Lane, the road to Stourbridge can be seen crossing the Stour and passing the gas works to begin its ascent of Dunsley, long before much of that area was completely built over.

The lane leading to Whittington and Cookley – wrongly captioned as Church Hill.

A seat provided a welcome rest for folk making the long climb up Church Hill, which even today has changed little.

From its hilltop position, the parish church dominates the village and its floodlit tower presents a dramatic and pleasing night-time scene. It is possible that, like so many hilltop sites, it could have been a place of pagan worship before the arrival of Christianity. It is known that there was a priest in Kinver in 1086, although no documentary record of a church building is apparent until the twelfth century. The church appears to have been rebuilt in the early fourteenth century as only a small amount of Norman stonework has survived. Over the past 600 years many alterations have been carried out, the biggest being in 1976 when the north aisle became structurally unsafe and was taken down. It was replaced to a design by Mr J.G. Smith of Kinver.

Glorious sunshine greeted the dedication of the church's new lych gate, the service being conducted by the Vicar, the Revd Thomas Cooper-Slipper.

The massive Victorian vicarage was eventually sold, and a modern vicarage took its place. In 2001 the old Vicarage was demolished to make way for apartment homes.

A house which still stands at the top of Meddins Lane and less than 200 yards from Kinver Edge, *c.* 1900. It was not long after the tourists began to arrive in their thousands that part of the ground floor was turned into a shop with its grounds becoming tea gardens. It offered cycle storage at *2d* per day. For generations it was known as 'Ison's'.

This photograph of, presumably, mother and daughter was actually a private greetings card. It is thought the property was in Foster Street.

This late nineteenth-century photograph is said to be of the Kinver Rifle Corps of the 35th Battalion of the Staffordshire Infantry. It was taken on top of Kinver Edge. Unfortunately there are no further details of the Corps or of its officers.

The dedication and consecration ceremony of the village war memorial to those killed during the First World War. The names of villagers killed in the Second World War were added to the original memorial, which stands on Kinver Edge. A second memorial was erected in the village in 2001.

Members of the parish church seen levelling ground in the 1920s in Vicarage Drive for the foundations of the church hall – a former First World War army hut. Second from the right is the Vicar, the Revd Thomas Cooper-Slipper.

A gang of workmen laying drainage pipes in Vicarage Drive.

Kinver's most famous daughter was Nancy Price, who was born in the village in 1880. Her father and grandfather were prosperous canal hauliers and her childhood home was Rockmount. She became one of England's most famous character actresses. Above she is starring in *Whiteoaks* and in several scenes she had her pet parrot perching on her shoulder. Left, she is Mrs D'Acquilar, with Cyril Keightley as Capt. Greville Satorys, in *The Whip*. Miss Price was awarded the CBE in 1950 for her services to the theatre and died in 1970 aged 90.

Kinver Boys' School, 1920s. When Edgecliff School was built in Castle Street the old school became Foley Infants. With a new infants' school later being built in Fairfield Drive, the old school was sold and was converted into a private residence in the 1970s.

Judging by the smart appearance of the children this could have been either an annual Sunday School 'treat' or a day out for the village schoolchildren – though where the event was held is not known.

Pupils of the National School at the turn of the last century.

This group photograph obviously had something to do with the parish church, and was taken outside the old parish church hall in the late 1920s. The vicar is seen on the extreme right.

All the schoolchildren of Kinver on a day out on Kinver Edge, 1920s.

Members of the Kinver School Garden Club hard at work overseen by their schoolmaster Mr Shepherd, 1913.

This photograph was obviously linked to some unidentified national celebrations, with 'John Bull' in the centre (and an English bull terrier in front of him). With such a variety of costumes and flags it may have been an Empire Day commemoration.

All smiles as the percussion band of Kinver Infants' School poses for the photographer, 1948.

Two widely differing jobs of work. Above, workmen celebrate the 'topping out' of the gas holder at Kinver Gas Works, while below a group of forestry workers are tree felling in Gibbet Wood, Dunsley.

A group of craftsmen at work in the closing years of the agricultural and spade works at The Hyde, *c*. 1910.

Whenever Kinver Carnival took place no effort was spared in decorating floats and creating costumes. Here a superbly dressed horse and trap (with ice cream) is about to join the procession.

The presence of the Vicar of Kinver, the Revd Thomas Cooper-Slipper on this photograph seems to indicate the football team was associated with the parish church. Unfortunately no details of the team or the players appeared with the undated photograph.

Yet another mystery picture. Where are the men working and what are they doing? The only identification on the photograph is the word 'Kinver'.

Kinver Sawmills with Mr Ken Wrigley (left) and a group of staff, *c*. 1930. The sawmills closed shortly after Mr Wrigley's death in 1996.

A scene on Kinver Wharf, where a horse is being tacked up for work, *c*. 1900. The wharf in question was below the lock, with an entrance track from Dunsley Road.

CHAPTER NINETEEN

LICENSED PREMISES

There was a time not so long ago when Kinver was well known for its 'real ale' pubs and was mentioned in the CAMRA *Real Ale Guide* as a place worth visiting. Mainly because of the number of round-the-year visitors the village had a larger number of pubs per head of population than many communities of a similar size. But in more recent times, owing mainly to drink driving laws, the number of pubs has decreased. However, this has been balanced to some extent by an increase in the number of licensed restaurants – several of which began life many years ago as traditional pubs.

The White Harte Hotel is the oldest licensed premises in the village, and has been licensed since 1605. Before the Kidderminster–Wolverhampton Road (A449) came into being, Kinver High Street carried the Bristol–Chester road and the White Harte was a coaching inn. Although Kinver had only the briefest involvement with the Civil War – there was a skirmish between the Royalist and Cromwellian forces at Stourbridge Heath – a Roundhead helmet was found in the White Harte during restoration work.

Probably the most historic house in Kinver Parish, other than Stourton Castle, is the Whittington Inn – or Ye Olde Whittington Inn. It was not until the eighteenth century that it became a hostelry. Prior to that it was the manor house of the De Whittingtons, having been built in about 1310. Richard, a grandson of the first owner, eventually became Lord Mayor of London (on four occasions); his undoubted aristocratic background destroys the pantomime legend of his going to London poor and penniless, with only his cat as company, and then making a fortune. Pictured below is the inn's grillroom, with its original inglenook fireplace.

Who these three gentlemen were at the entrance to the Whittington is not recorded, but many famous people must have passed through the doorway. Lady Jane Grey lived there as a child and her ghost is said still to roam the corridors. King Charles II is said to have called there on his flight from Worcester; in 1711 Queen Anne visited and, as was her custom when staying overnight, left her iron seal (since stolen) on the door.

The first pub that passengers off the trams saw was The Stag in Mill Lane. Its beer was said to be amongst the best in the village, for it was stored in sandstone caves at the rear of the building. This photograph was probably something of a joke for its portrays a group of regulars partaking of a jug of ale with snow on the ground in the winter of 1905. The licensee at the time was John Roberts – but who the two barmaids were (below) is not recorded.

An old picture of the Vine Inn. The licensee at the time was Benjamin Hadley shown here with a group of customers, *c.* 1900.

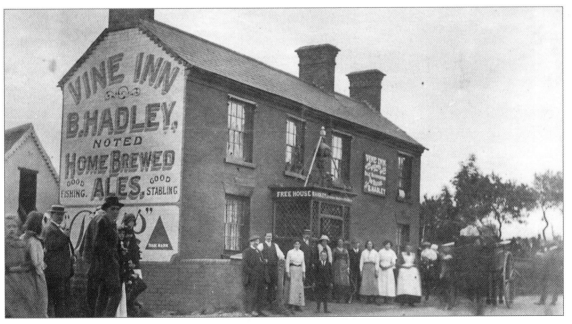

A later photograph of the Vine Inn. The tree in front of one of the windows has been removed. Again there is no record of the photograph commemorating a particular event. At the side of the premises there was a cart track leading to a coal wharf; in later years the wharf became part of the pub's beer gardens.

The Vine Inn's Bowls Club at the turn of the century (above). Thirty-five years on (below) and the regulars pose as the 'Lads of the Vine'. The only lady present was presumably the licensee's wife.

At one time Ye Olde Plough at the bottom of Stone Lane was one of Kinver's most popular pubs. The whole of the bar area was decorated with a huge variety of brassware including some old horse brasses. But over the years the pub lost its popularity, and after a period of dwindling trade it closed. It was demolished in 1996–7 and replaced by private housing.

Out of the village a major landmark was the Stewponey and Foley Arms Hotel, situated at the junction of the Stourbridge–Bridgnorth and Kidderminster–Wolverhampton main roads.

Because of its situation the Stewponey was also a popular overnight stop for long-distance travellers and a drinking haven for boatmen on the adjacent canal. It gained even more trade when the Kinver Light Railway opened. Pictured below, some years later, are a group of patrons who had arrived by motor coach.

The Stewponey & Foley Arms Hotel as it was in the early 1900s (above) and in the 1930s (below) when the original hotel was being demolished to make way for the 'road house' hotel at the rear. The new complex also included an open air unheated swimming pool with the imposing title of the Stewponey Lido. When it was demolished in 2002 to make way for a housing development there was a public outcry as the hotel was the last remaining example of a 1930s road house.

This badly faded photograph was found in an album in a junk shop. Dated 1887, it is of the Cross Inn at the corner of Dark Lane. While the main structure is virtually unchanged, the front garden and side gardens are now a car park.

This token was discovered in a Black Country bric-a-brac shop. Bearing the name 'White Hart Hotel, Kinver', nothing is known of its origin other than that the R.M. Neale mentioned was Raglan Neale, licensee of the hotel in the late nineteenth century and a parish councillor. Whether he had other business interests in Kinver and issued this token to his employees, or merely to employees in the hotel, is not known.

CHAPTER TWENTY

PRESTWOOD

In the seventeenth century Prestwood was home to the prosperous Halfcot Wire Works. According to *Stewponey Countryside* by Francis E. Cambell the works also had its own workers' cottages, while a small sandstone building was provided which not only served as a school but was also used as a Sunday school and church. The works' premises and land were sold on 23 June 1829.

In 1850 the day school was built by Mr J.H.H. Foley. It also held church services, and when the Foley Estates were sold in 1913 Mr Francis Grazebrook of Stourton Castle bought the church and presented it to the Lichfield Diocese. The day school was closed following the 1885 Education Act, although Sunday services, conducted by the lay reader (Headmaster of Kinver Grammar School), continued for some years. When the last headmaster of the Grammar School died, Alderman H.S. Walker of Stourbridge took over as Lay Reader in Charge. The building has now been converted to a private residence.

Prestwood Day School.

This newly widened and apparently quiet road of the early 1930s is now the busy A449 trunk road at Prestwood. The building on the right is the Stourton Locks Cottage, which was owned by the Stourbridge Navigation Company and occupied by the keeper of the four Stourton Locks. Records show that some 150 years ago the lock keeper received substantial extra payments for being on duty at times for up to twenty-four hours a day, such was the volume of traffic through the locks.

This house was built as the new lodge house at the entrance of the drive to the Prestwood Sanatorium in the early 1920s.

Described on this postcard as the County Sanatorium, Prestwood, this building stood on the site of the former Prestwood House. At a time when recovery from tuberculosis was none too common, medical thinking was that the fresh woodland air of Prestwood was an aid to recovery. The origins of Prestwood House have been traced back to the reign of Richard III when it was occupied by John De Somery. It is believed that before then the area was associated with members of a monastic order based at Wolverhampton. As a private house it was occupied and structurally added to by many famous local families, among them the Dudleys, Lytteltons, Sebrights, Hodgsons and Foleys. The area is now occupied by a private nursing home.

The belief that the best chance of a cure for tuberculosis included unlimited amounts of fresh air was the reason for the construction of a large number of individual chalets for all but the most seriously affected of patients. These two pictures record the building and completion of the Prestwood Sanatorium chalets.

The sanatorium was supported by public donations and various other acts of charity by many groups and local authorities throughout the Black Country. One such group was this concert party which entertained patients. One of the senior nursing staff is seen in the doorway.

Employees of Prestwood Estate also formed the estate's fire brigade and here they are pictured with some of their equipment. It is possible the brigade was formed after Enville Hall was almost totally destroyed by fire.

The large country houses of the period all had large number of domestic staff. Here the staff of Prestwood House are seen with the head butler.

CHAPTER TWENTY-ONE

TOURISM

From early Victorian times there is evidence that Kinver was a tourist venue for the more prosperous who could afford to own or hire horse-drawn transport; the alternative was a walk of at least 4 miles from Stourbridge or the use of primitive cycles.

When the Kinver Light Railway opened, thousands of Black Country folk descended on the village every week during the summer period. A number of residents quickly transformed front rooms or converted their gardens and outhouses into tea rooms while others, with larger houses, entered the bed and breakfast market.

In 1902 a wave of optimism that Kinver was about to join the tourist trade big-time led to one of its oldest public houses, Ye Olde Green Dragon (first licensed in 1718), being demolished and replaced with a three-storey up-market hotel. But the expected influx of paying guests failed to materialise because most visitors were daytrippers. In 1936 the Green Dragon went out of business and was converted into what is now the Constitutional Club.

For the past hundred years the village has been a popular destination and tourism is now important throughout the year. A wide variety of licensed restaurants coupled with many miles of forest and heathland walks on and around Kinver Edge offer a pleasant and healthier alternative to more artificial and costly tourist venues.

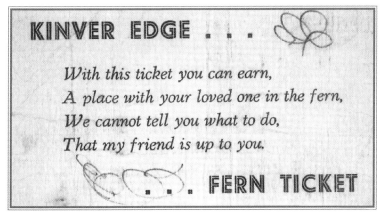

KINVER EDGE . . .

With this ticket you can earn,
A place with your loved one in the fern,
We cannot tell you what to do,
That my friend is up to you.

. . . FERN TICKET

Apart from being a popular area for family outings Kinver's country lanes and secluded areas of woodland were favourite areas for courting couples. It was not long before some enterprising shopkeeper in the village – no names, no pack drill! – produced and sold considerable numbers of extremely 'saucy' (for those days) Kinver Edge Fern Tickets. What parents said when they found these tickets in their offspring's pockets is best left to the imagination.

Edge View Hotel was a prize example of a good idea that went badly wrong. Shortly after the Kinver Light Railway opened and began bringing in thousands of visitors, the hotel was built in the Compa. Apart from luxurious rooms, the hotel also operated the Café Royale tea rooms which had seating for over 300 people. But the enterprise eventually went bankrupt; blame for its failure was levelled at the local licensing magistrates who steadfastly refused to grant it permission to sell alcohol – even though in the village there were premises, such as Ye Olde Green Dragon Hotel, that were fully licensed. It then became a sanatorium linked to the existing sanatorium at Prestwood. After tuberculosis was virtually eradicated it was used as a convalescent and recovery home. Another change of use saw it as a home for mentally handicapped people. In the 1970s it was closed but eventually reopened in recent years as a residential care home.

To reach the summit of Kinver Edge from the village, visitors had to walk along some steep and heavily wooded lanes. One such route was here at Church Hill. Once on the edge there were panoramic views, including this one of the Edge, with the former Edge View Hotel in the valley.

The sylvan beauty of the slopes of Kinver Edge is captured in this 1904 view of what is captioned merely as 'Forest, Kinver.'

A postcard scene of Kingsford Lane, *c.* 1904.

An early postcard view of the Rock Houses, *c.* 1910.

Kinver Edge, 1920.

This impressive looking gentleman is Mr Vizard who lived in Foster Street, Kinver, and was famed for his enormous telescope. He used, it is said, to pay local lads a penny or two to drag a small cart carrying the equipment on to Kinver Edge. He then used to charge visitors 'a penny a look'. The telescope by all accounts had tremendous magnification and afforded clear and detailed views of a vast area between Dudley Top Church, the Clee Hills and the Malverns. It proved quite an attraction. Apparently he ran this enterprise for some years, and also built himself a shelter on the Edge! It is said the telescope came off a First World War battleship.

Three old tramcar bodies found new homes as a popular café and tea room in the Compa. Seating was also installed on the roofs, although such a facility may have been a left-over from when they were in service.

On the opposite side of the Compa to the 'tramcar tea rooms' were Martindale's Tea Gardens, next to which were the Compa Cottage Tea Gardens with a sign 'school parties specially catered for'. The horse-drawn delivery cart was owned by Mr Walker who had a general stores in the village. The picture above was taken in about 1900, while the postcard view below was taken some twenty years later.

By the time this card was sold by C.E. Grove to a visitor from Lincolnshire in 1932 it was already some ten years old. It shows another scene of the cluster of cafés in the Compa.

The major 'tourist draw' of Kinver was the Rock Houses, many of which were occupied. The Rock House museum was a former rock house that Mr Fairbridge had converted. He ran it for some twenty years complete with a selection of penny amusement machines.

Afternoon tea at the Rock House Café (Holy Austin Rock). This photograph was taken after the last war and already the area was becoming overgrown.

The caves of Nanny's Rock were favourite playgrounds for children, but in the 1950s they were the source of complaints by local people because of the late night parties that young people held there.

Regrettably there is no identification of either the woman or the boy pictured outside the Crow's Rock House.

Visitors pictured (above) at the side of
Crow's Rock in this 1912 postcard view.
The photograph right is similar to that on
the previous page of the unnamed woman
at Crow's Rock House; on this occasion
she was pictured with a younger boy.

A view of Holy Austin Rock, *c.* 1905 (above), and a view of the same location, *c.* 1920 (below). In the intervening years the tree on top of the rock had been removed while tree growth in the gardens had increased. In both pictures the presence of tea rooms was prominently advertised. In the lower picture a range of penny amusement machines can be seen to the left of the houses.

Three visitors take a break on Nanny's Rock.

Quite what the point was of this postcard view from inside the Rock House Museum will forever
remain a mystery.

The Rock Houses at Holy Austin Rock were built on two levels and stories are still told that the families on the top level regarded themselves as 'above' those on the lower level in more ways than one! This picture of a house on the bottom level was the setting for the 1919 film *Bladys of the Stewponey*, which was financed by Kinver resident and Black Country industrialist Benjamin Priest. An unusual feature of this dwelling is that the chimney brickwork from the living-room fire and oven follows the contour of the cliff face.

This lady was probably the most photographed of all the rock house residents. She is pictured (above) at the well-head outside one of the 'bottom level' houses, *c.* 1910. This house was lived in by Mr and Mrs Fletcher in 1900 and they are featured in a painting by Mr Alfred Rushton, which now hangs in the Constitutional Club, Kinver.

Above, the same well-head, same lady, but with the photographer in a different place! The picture below was taken a few years later, the only major change to the scene being the renewed wooden frame at the well-head.

For much of the journey down Kingsford
Lane out of Kinver Parish and towards
Wolverley the sandstone cliffs were a regular
feature of the landscape. Although the cliff
faces are now hidden by thick undergrowth
and trees, traces of rock houses can still be
found. These are two such dwellings close to
where the underground wartime factory was
built at Drakelow. When these two pictures
(taken it is believed at the turn of the last
century) appeared in a magazine, they were
captioned 'The Troglodytes of Blakeshall
Common'. As they were well off the tourist
'beat' and set back some distance from
Kingsford Lane they remained as private
dwellings.

Another of the 'bottom level' houses at Holy Austin Rock. Note the spelling of Austen; on many postcards it was spelt 'Austin'.

Homeward-bound visitors head for the tram terminus in Mill Lane, *c.* 1905. Local residents were obviously cashing in on the tourist trade with roadside refreshment and gift stalls. The cottage on the right displays a cycle storage sign. Beyond is The Stag inn.

Sadly these distinctive almshouses were demolished in the 1960s (despite strong local opposition) to make way for the characterless façades of modern shops. Today such a clearance scheme would be unthinkable.

Kinver High Street, 1916. The villas on the left were all offering refreshments, apartments and cycle storage. Beyond them is Ye Olde Green Dragon Hotel while to the right are Kemp's Tea Rooms.

Trams wait at the terminus for the homeward-bound rush, *c.* 1905. The all-time record for passenger numbers was the Whitsuntide Bank Holiday Monday and Tuesday of 1905 when the line carried over 31,000 people to the village in a thirty-hour period. Contemporary reports tell of a long queue of passengers stretching back into the High Street; every available single-deck tram (double deckers were forbidden to use the line) was in service, and they ran at seven minute intervals. It was well into the evening before the last of the visitors had departed. There were even occasional buskers serenading folk on their way.

Visitors also came by motor coach in later years. An all-male party is pictured outside the Vine Inn. The event must have been special for most of the party were wearing buttonholes. The coach, a Daimler, may have been operated by Samuel Johnson of Stourbridge. An interesting feature of the Vine Inn for several years was the wooden carving of bunches of grapes above the entrance porch.

I am thinking of You at

KINVER

Like all holiday haunts, Kinver had a selection of 'comic' cards. It is interesting that many featured a man smoking – such was the social and leisure appeal of a cigarette in those days. Here then is a small selection of those cards – some of which command quite high prices among collectors.

KINVER.

Time somehow seems to fly at Kinver — come and test it.

Tens of thousands of 'comic' cards were posted from Kinver between 1900 and the early 1930s, the boom years of day-tripping. Produced in the early years of colour printing, they proved a popular alternative to more traditional photographic cards.

We go the Pace at KINVER

In our fine motor car we can
  go near and far,
The sights of the country
  admiring;
And we carry behind 'neath
  our motor confined
The beauties we think
  most inspiring.

Our Landlord at Kinver
is very obliging

Cards were printed by firms in London and locally. They were produced to a standard design and the word 'Kinver' was then added in the appropriate place. In this example the printer has not quite lined up the words properly.

As with postcards, so it was with cheap pottery souvenirs of a visit to Kinver. There were literally hundreds of different items produced over a period of around thirty years yet surprisingly few seem to have survived. Those that have are highly sought after by collectors. Most of the pottery souvenirs of Kinver were made by Crest Ware whose factory was at Platts Crescent, Amblecote.

The bulk of the gifts were made for Jennings' shop in Kinver High Street.

Not only subjects of local interest (top and left) but also favourite fictional characters of the day (above) were depicted on popular tourist gifts.

CHAPTER TWENTY-TWO

ENVILLE

T he casual visitor or passing motorist could be forgiven for thinking that Enville is a community that time has almost forgotten. Apart from the occasional modern property and the busy Bridgnorth road which cuts through the village, Enville's appearance has changed little in the past hundred years.

It owes its escape from the spread of suburbia to the surrounding Green Belt land and the fact that much of the area lies within the vast estate of Enville Hall and is a conservation area.

Enville is entirely rural, with its parish including many isolated farms and cottages – the latter reflecting their origins as homes for workers in the Kinver Forest and the woodlands of the Enville Hall estate.

Like Kinver, Enville is an ancient settlement and once comprised three manors – the Anglo-Saxon settlements of Enville and Morfe with the third manor, Lutley, being first mentioned in the twelfth century.

Ownership of Enville Hall has remained in the same family for 470 years, and the Hall is still the focal point of the village.

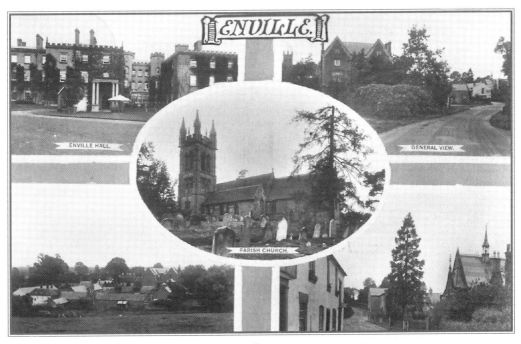

Enville views.

Years ago the economic welfare of Enville village was almost entirely dependent on the Hall and its vast estate of farms and forestry. Most of the inhabitants either worked on the estate or were retired employees. For 470 years the Hall has remained in the same family, since Sir Edward Grey of Whittington bought the manor from Lord Dudley in 1528. It eventually became the home of the Earls of Stamford and Warrington. When the title became extinct in 1883, ownership of the manor was passed down through the female line.

Mopping-up operations in progress at Enville Hall after the disastrous fire on 25 November 1904 which gutted most of the central part of the building. The horse-drawn steam-powered pump seen in action here was one of two which made a hazardous seven mile journey along ice- and snow-bound roads from Stourbridge. The fire brigade had been summoned by a Hall employee who cycled in pitch darkness in the early hours of the morning to Stourbridge to raise the alarm.

So fierce was the fire that the two Stourbridge pumps plus the Hall's own hand-operated pump (it took twelve men to operate it) pumped over 1,000 gallons of water an hour from the Sea Horse Pool for nearly twenty-four hours. A contemporary report of the event stated: 'The fire continued to burn for three days and smouldered for two weeks.' The cause of the fire was never precisely established but it was thought to have spread from a chimney fire in one of the guest bedrooms, which was being prepared for a shooting and house party the next day.

Enville Parish Church, perched on a hill behind the village, dominates the skyline. Architectural evidence has indicated that a church existed on this site in the twelfth century. Today's church was substantially restored internally and externally between 1872 and 1874.

Years ago church unity was not a strong point in the village. Nonconformity in the form of Wesleyan Methodism began to flourish and in 1855 a house was in use as a chapel. But about two years later Methodism suddenly disappeared following fierce opposition from the Rector, Cornelius Jesson. Whether the house was owned by the Hall and the Rector had exerted pressure in that direction is not known.

Pupils of the Church of England village school with their headmaster Mr England.

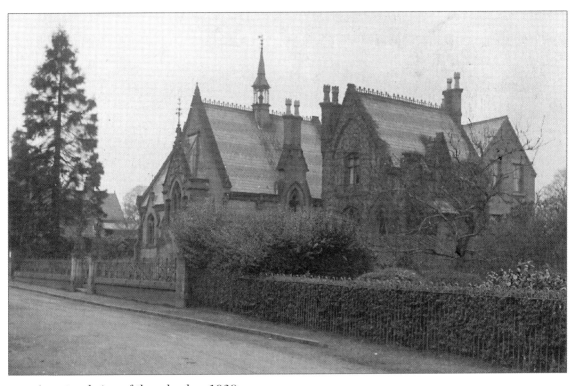

A postcard view of the school, *c.* 1920.

Two farming scenes in Enville. Above, a pair of horses led by Bill Giles and below, a cartload of sacks of grain and a team of three horses led by Charles Giles. Information with the photograph said the grain was destined for Sutton Coldfield.

Employees of the Hall gardens and farm staff pose for a group photograph.

A group of land workers harvesting carrots in the 1920s. Among them are John Mills, Mr Avery, George Mills, Alec Wright and Charles Avery.

Beetroot being harvested in one of the market gardens. One of the staff is named as Alan Bullock.

Chapel Cottage garden with the owner Mrs Reynolds (left) and an unnamed helper. Was this the cottage in which the short-lived Methodist society held their meetings?

A view of Enville Hall from the gardens, with the Sea Horse Pool in the middle distance. In the early nineteenth century the gardens and lakes were nationally renowned and attracted up to 8,000 visitors a year who arrived in specially hired horse 'brakes', their own carriages or on foot from miles around. The fountains of the Sea Horse Pool were gravity fed from a reservoir on high ground, to which water was supplied through two steam-powered pumps. As it happened the pool could not have been better placed for it provided an ample supply of water during the fire of 1904.

There were many attractions in the Hall's grounds. Above are the immaculately tended yew hedges and flower beds, leading to an ornate summer house. Part of a large complex of greenhouses can be seen behind the hedge. Left, is a rare (though faded) picture of a highly decorative building. A scribbled note on the reverse describes it as 'Enville Museum'.

Highlight of the splendour of Enville Hall gardens and parkland was the magnificent and ornate conservatory, which housed exotic specimen plants from around the world. It was built in 1855 and was described by one commentator as 'second only to Crystal Palace'.

Maintenance of the conservatory, gardens and parkland was an immense undertaking and over thirty staff were in full-time employment.

The first major landscaping work was designed and supervised by the poet and landscape designer William Shenstone of Halesowen, whose work was later commemorated by the building of Shenstone's Chapel on the edge of the woodland. Over the years further landscaping was carried out and eventually the area was so large that a carriage road was installed to enable visitors to travel through it.

The conservatory was demolished in 1927. The work was carried out by Sadler's of Stourbridge, who were also responsible for the demolition of the Foley residence at Prestwood following a fire.

Enville's 'Dad's Army'. The Enville and District Home Guard company photographed at Enville Golf Club House, 1942.

ACKNOWLEDGEMENTS

The authors gratefully acknowledge the assistance of Mr David Bills, President of Kinver Historical Society, for his unlimited patience in double-checking the innumerable historical facts that emerged in the production of the text accompanying the photographs, and for allowing access to the Society's comprehensive archives. We also thank Miss J. White and Kinver Library, Peter Allsopp, Anthony Phipps and Mr A.J. Mills for the loan of photographs.

KINVER HISTORICAL SOCIETY

For many years Kinver has had a thriving Historical Society. It meets on the first Wednesday of the month at the Senior Citizens Club, High Street, Kinver. Its programme includes authoritative presentations by a wide variety of experts on various aspects of local and Black Country heritage with occasional visits to locations of historic importance. Details of the Society are available from the President, Mr David Bills, of The Pharmacy, High Street, Kinver. The authors ask readers to bear in mind that the Society would be pleased to receive into its care any material – photographs or documents – relating to the village's development over the centuries.

KINVER CIVIC SOCIETY

Normally civic societies are found in towns and cities, but such is the pride in the history and heritage of Kinver and the interest in the future well being of the village and its environs that the area has its own Society which enjoys a strong membership. Over the years it has made numerous awards to organisations and individuals for collective and individual efforts towards the betterment of the community and parish. The Society meets at the Kinver Community Centre on the third Monday of the month. Details are available from The Pharmacy, High Street, Kinver.